WE DRINK FROM
OUR OWN WELLS

WE DRINK FROM OUR OWN WELLS

THE SPIRITUAL JOURNEY OF A PEOPLE

Gustavo Gutiérrez

Translated from the Spanish by
Matthew J. O'Connell

ORBIS BOOKS
Maryknoll, New York

DOVE COMMUNICATIONS
Melbourne, Australia

Fourth Printing, July 1985

The Catholic Foreign Mission Society of America (Maryknoll) recruits and trains people for overseas missionary service. Through Orbis Books Maryknoll aims to foster the international dialogue that is essential to mission. The books published, however, reflect the opinions of their authors and are not meant to represent the official position of the society.

Except where otherwise indicated, Bible quotations are from the Revised Standard Version.

First published as *Beber en su propio pozo: En el itinerario espiritual de un pueblo,* second edition, revised, by Centro de Estudios y Publicaciones (CEP), Jirón Lampa 808, of. 601, Apdo. 6118, Lima, Peru, copyright © 1983 by Gustavo Gutiérrez

English translation copyright © 1984 by Orbis Books, Maryknoll, NY 10545
Published in the United States of America by Orbis Books, Maryknoll, NY 10545
Published in Australia by Dove Communications, Box 316 Blackburn, Victoria 3130

Manufactured in the United States of America

Manuscript Editor: William E. Jerman

Library of Congress Cataloging in Publication Data
Gutiérrez, Gustavo, 1928-
  We drink from our own wells.

  Translation of: Beber de su propio pozo.
  Includes bibliographical references.
  1. Latin America—Religious life and customs.
2. Spiritual life. 3. Latin America—Economic
conditions—1945- . 4. Church and the poor.
I. Title.
BR600.G8713   1984   209'.8   83-22008
ISBN 0-88344-707-X (pbk.)

DOVE ISBN 0-85924-308-7

To Luis Vallejos
and
Luis Dalle,
bishops who devoted
their lives
to sharing the faith
and hope
of the peoples of the
Andes.
Friends forever.

Bibet de fonte putei sui primus ipse.
—St. Bernard of Clairvaux,
De consideratione

CONTENTS

ABBREVIATIONS   xi

FOREWORD, *by Henri J. M. Nouwen*   xiii

INTRODUCTION   1

Part One
How Shall We Sing to the Lord in a Foreign Land?   7

1. IN A FOREIGN LAND   9
   An Alien World   9
   Questions   13
   New Wine in Old Bottles   16

2. THE SONG OF THE POOR   19
   A Favorable Time   20
   Toward a New Spirituality   25

Part Two
Here There Is No Longer Any Way   33

3. ENCOUNTER WITH THE LORD   35
   Spirituality and Theology   35
   See, Touch, Follow   38
   Acknowledging the Messiah   45
   Encounter, Experience, Reflection, Prolongation   52

4. WALKING ACCORDING TO THE SPIRIT   54
   The Flesh of Death   55
   The Spirit of Life   61
   The Resurrection Body   64

5. A PEOPLE IN SEARCH OF GOD   72
   The Spirituality of a People   73
   A Manner of Being a Christian   83

Part Three
Free to Love   *91*

6. CONVERSION: A REQUIREMENT FOR
   SOLIDARITY   95
   Break and Solidarity   96
   The Material and the Spiritual   102
   Consistency and Stubbornness   104

7. GRATUITOUSNESS:
   THE ATMOSPHERE FOR EFFICACY   107
   Efficacious Love   107
   Everything Is Grace   109
   A Twofold Movement   112

8. JOY: VICTORY OVER SUFFERING   114
   Schooling in Martyrdom   115
   Easter Joy   117

9. SPIRITUAL CHILDHOOD:
   A REQUIREMENT FOR COMMITMENT TO THE
   POOR   122
   With the Poor and against Poverty   123
   The World of the Poor   124
   Spiritual Childhood   126

10. COMMUNITY: OUT OF SOLITUDE   128
   The Dark Night of Injustice   129
   Living in Community   131

CONCLUSION   136

NOTES   138

INDEX OF SCRIPTURAL REFERENCES   173

INDEX OF NAMES AND SOURCES   177

ABBREVIATIONS

DTC   *Dictionnaire de théologie catholique*

JB   *Jerusalem Bible*

PD   Puebla Document ("Final Document of the Third General Conference of the Latin American Episcopate"), in John Eagleson and Philip Scharper, eds., *Puebla and Beyond* (Maryknoll, N.Y.: Orbis, 1979), pp. 122–285.

SL   *Signos de liberación: Testimonios de la Iglesia en América latina, 1969–1973* (Lima: CEP, 1973).

SLE   *Signos de lucha y esperanza: Testimonios de la Iglesia en América latina, 1973–1978* (Lima: CEP, 1978).

SVF   *Signos de vida y fidelidad: Testimonios de la Iglesia en América latina, 1978–1982* (Lima: CEP, 1983).

FOREWORD

A significant event in the development of liberation theology is the publication of *We Drink from Our Own Wells: The Spiritual Journey of a People* by Gustavo Gutiérrez. Gustavo's book fulfills the promise that was implicit in his *A Theology of Liberation* which appeared in Spanish in 1971 and soon became a charter for many Latin American theologians and pastoral workers.

In that earlier work, Gustavo was already speaking of the need for and the importance of a spirituality of liberation. He realized from the beginning that a theology that does not come out of an authentic encounter with the Lord can never be fruitful. In 1971, he wrote: "Where oppression and the liberation of man seem to make God irrelevant—a God filtered by our longtime indifference to these problems—there must blossom faith and hope in Him who comes to root out injustice and to offer, in an unforeseen way, total liberation."

More than ten years were to pass before Gustavo had the opportunity to develop this spirituality fully, but it was worth waiting for. *We Drink from Our Own Wells* is the nuanced articulation of the Christ-encounter as experienced by the poor of Latin America in their struggle to affirm their human dignity and claim their true identity as sons and daughters of God. As in all true spiritualities, this spirituality of liberation is deeply rooted in the lived experience of God's presence in history, an experience that is as unique and new for the poor in Latin America as it was for St. Benedict, St. Francis of Assisi, St. Ignatius Loyola, and their followers.

The Rev. Henri J. M. Nouwen has written many books on spirituality, including *¡Gracias!*, a description of his six-month pastoral experience in Latin America. This foreword first appeared in *America,* October 15, 1983, and is here used with permission.

The title of this new book expresses the core idea it describes. St. Bernard of Clairvaux's observation, "Everyone has to drink from his own well," raises the question: "From what well can the poor of Latin America drink?" It is obviously that unique and renewing encounter with the living Christ in the struggle for freedom. "Spirituality," Gustavo writes, "is like living water that springs up in the very depths of the experience of faith." To drink from your own well is to live your own life in the Spirit of Jesus as you have encountered him in your concrete historical reality. This has nothing to do with abstract opinions, convictions, or ideas, but it has everything to do with the tangible, audible, and visible experience of God, an experience so real that it can become the foundation of a life project. As the First Epistle of John puts it: "What we have heard, what we have seen with our eyes, what we have looked upon and our hands have touched—we speak of the word of life."

I must confess that my conviction about the importance of Gustavo's book is older than the book itself. In Lima, during 1982, I attended the course in which Gustavo first presented the main themes of a spirituality of liberation. I remember this course as one of the most significant experiences of my six-month stay in Latin America—not simply because of what was said but also, and even more, because of how it was received. I was part of an unusual learning event in which approximately 2,000 "pastoral agents" participated. These people had come not only from all the districts of Peru but also from Chile, Brazil, Colombia, Paraguay, Uruguay, Argentina, Panama, and Nicaragua. They made a youthful, vital, enthusiastic student body that recognized in Gustavo's words its own deepest soul. The spirituality that was described for these Latin American Christians was not perceived as an alien or an imported way of thinking but as an expression of what they had already come to know in their daily living of the gospel.

My own sense of the importance of *We Drink from Our Own Wells* comes from having been with these young men and women who had lived the Latin American reality and had there encountered the Lord and drunk from the fountains of living water flowing from within him. Most of these students were born and raised in poor barrios and had become active pastoral agents in the process of liberation. They knew their own people and had learned to think with one eye on the gospel and one eye on the painful reality they shared with these people. They worked in their various districts and countries as catechists, social workers, or project coordinators. They were all deeply immersed in the Bible and had come to think of themselves as the people of God called to the promised land. They knew it would be a long, arduous, and often painful journey, but the encounter with their Lord had given them the strength to be faithful in the struggle even when immediate results were not visible.

When Gustavo explained that the spiritual journey would not be a journey from nothing to something but a journey in which they had already met the One for whom they were searching, it was clear that his audience understood what he was talking about. The way in which these young Christians spoke about their Lord was so direct and fearless that it became clear that their pastoral work among the poor was not based on any mere idea or theory but on a deep, personal experience of the presence of a loving God in the midst of the struggle for justice and peace. There was joy and gratitude; there was warm friendship and generosity; there was humility and mutual care, and these gifts were received from the Lord who had called them to be his witnesses among a suffering people.

In this course, given during the Peruvian summertime, Gustavo's spirituality came alive for me precisely through those who were receiving it with open mind and eager heart. I would now like to explore in more detail some aspects of this spirituality of liberation. To do this, I shall not only make use of the ideas expressed in *W. Drink from Our Own Wells*, but also recall the way in which these ideas were received by men and women who have committed themselves to pastoral ministry in Latin America.

The spirituality of liberation touches every dimension of life. It is a truly biblical spirituality that allows God's saving act in history to penetrate all levels of human existence. God is seen here as the God of the living who enters into humanity's history to dispel the forces of death, wherever they are at work, and to call forth the healing and reconciling forces of life. It is precisely in the context of the struggle of the Latin American poor that the powers of death have become visible. "Poverty means death," Gustavo writes. This death, however, is not only physical but mental and cultural as well. It refers to the destruction of individual persons, peoples, cultures, and traditions. In Latin America, the poor and marginalized have become more and more aware that these forces of death have made them strangers in their own land. They recognize more clearly the ways in which they are bound by hostility, fear, and manipulation, and they have gradually come to understand the evil structures that victimize them. With this new self-consciousness, the poor have broken into history and have rediscovered that the God whom they have worshiped for centuries is not a God who wants their poverty but a God who wants to liberate them from those forces of death and offer them life in all its dimensions.

This spirituality, as Gustavo articulates it, makes it impossible to reduce liberation theology to a political movement. The struggle to which the God of the Bible calls his people is much larger than a struggle for political or economic rights. It is a struggle against all the forces of death wherever they become manifest and a struggle for life in the fullest sense.

But as I reflect on the impact of this spirituality on my own way of living and thinking, I realize that a reductionism has taken place on my side. Talking with those pastoral workers during that summer course, I became aware of how individualistic and elitist my own spirituality had been. It was hard to confess, but true, that in many respects my thinking about the spiritual life had been deeply influenced by my North American milieu with its emphasis upon the "interior life" and the methods and techniques for developing that life. Only when I confronted what Gustavo calls the "irruption of the poor into history" did I become aware of how "spiritualized" my spirituality had become. It had been, in fact, a spirituality for introspective persons who have the luxury of the time and space needed to develop inner harmony and quietude. I had even read the Gospels in a rather romantic way. I had come to pray the Magnificat as a sweet song of Mary. I had come to look at the children in the New Testament as innocent, harmless beings, and I had come to think of humility, faithfulness, obedience, and purity primarily as forms of personal piety.

But the spirituality of *We Drink from Our Own Wells* does not allow such reductionism. The poor in Latin America have made us realize that living as Christians in our contemporary world, with an open eye and an open heart for the real problems of people, challenges us to break out of our individualism and elitism and start listening to the Bible with new ears. The poor help us recognize the power of the words of Mary's song: "He has deposed the mighty from their thrones and raised the lowly to high places." They also help us see that the children who were touched by Jesus were the forgotten ones, and they help us rediscover the social dimension of humility, faithfulness, obedience and purity.

A second crucial aspect of the spirituality of liberation is its Christ-centeredness. Gustavo begins his book with the words: "A Christian is defined as a follower of Jesus," and he dedicates the core chapter of this work to an exploration of those opening words. Those who do not grasp the centrality of Jesus in the struggle for full human freedom will always misinterpret liberation theology as well as liberation spirituality. Gustavo pays careful attention to the intimate encounters with Jesus that are recorded in the New Testament. All discipleship, he emphasizes, is rooted in these most personal encounters, and the messianic community is formed from them. The disciples recognize Jesus as the Messiah and thus become part of a community destined to give testimony to God's kingdom in the midst of the concreteness of human history.

It is here that the profound importance of a liberation spirituality as the undergirding of a liberation theology becomes clear. Those who see in liberation theology a theological rationale for a class struggle in which the poor claim their rights and try to break the power of their oppressors have ignored the center of the struggle for freedom. Jesus is the center. Jesus the Lord loves the oppressor as well as the oppressed and entered into history to set all men and women free. Knowing Jesus in the way the disciples knew him does not allow for a cool and calculated strategy aimed at the overthrow of the oppressor and the acquistion of power by the poor. The good news that Jesus announces is the news that love is stronger than death and that the evils of hatred, destruction, exploitation, and oppression can only be overcome by the power of love that comes from God.

In his lectures, even more than in his book, Gustavo stressed the importance of warm, affectionate, and caring relationships among those who struggle for and with the poor. Those who can say, "We have encountered the Messiah," are not fighting for a far-off cause, nor are they forming groups because of a common fear of an enemy or a common desire for power. On the contrary, their struggle is already won. By encountering the Lord they already possess that for which they strive, already taste that for which they hunger. By their struggle they aim to make fully visible a victory over death that has already been accomplished. This makes possible a community life that is one of joy, peace, and true love.

Gustavo points out that the initiative for the encounter with Christ comes from the Lord himself. To those who ask, "Where do you live?" Jesus answers, "Come and see," and later he directly invites them to become his followers. Discipleship is first and foremost the response to an invitation. This insight is essential for an understanding of the spirituality of liberation. Some have accused liberation theology of Pelagianism as though it called upon people to redeem the world themselves. Nothing is farther from the truth. In *We Drink from Our Own Wells*, Gustavo avoids any suggestion that the world's salvation depends on our efforts. It is precisely the gratuitous quality of God's love, revealed in Jesus, that sets us free to work in the service of God's kingdom.

As one who has been exposed to many styles of theological liberalism, I am struck by the orthodoxy of this Christ-centered spirituality. It is solidly rooted in the teachings of the ecumenical councils. The Christians of Latin America, as Gustavo himself once pointed out to me, came to a realization of the social dimensions of their faith without going through a modernistic phase. He used Archbishop Romero as a striking example. Through his direct contact with the suffering people, that traditional churchman became a social critic without ever rejecting, or even criticizing, his traditional past. In fact, Archbishop Romero's traditional understanding of God's presence in history was the basis and source of his courageous protest against the exploitation and oppression of the people of El Salvador. A similar quality is characteristic of Gustavo's spirituality which is fed by the age-old Trinitarian faith of the church and by the religious experiences of the great saints who incorporated that faith in their lives.

A third aspect of the spirituality developed in *We Drink from*

Our Own Wells is its inductive character. By that I mean that this spirituality is drawn from the concrete daily experiences of the Christian communities in Latin America. "The fact is," Gustavo writes, "that daily contact with the experiences of some, a reading of the writings of many, and the testimony of still others have convinced me of the profound spiritual experiences that persons among us are living today."

The third and final section of *We Drink from Our Own Wells* is filled with deeply moving texts written by Christian men and women who have experienced persecution and suffering but have been witnesses to the living and hope-giving God in the midst of their sufferings. From these testimonies we can indeed see that "something new is being born . . . in Latin America."

Gustavo has not simply written another book about the spiritual life. For many years he participated with his whole being in the painful struggle of his people. Out of this intimate solidarity he was able to identify the traits of a new spirituality, traits that he could read in the faces of the people with whom he lived. The words he chose for these traits belong to the treasury of the Christian spiritual tradition: conversion, gratuity, joy, spiritual childhood, and community.

But these old words sound fresh and new when they have been distilled from the life experience of the suffering Latin American church. Conversion then emerges as part of a process of solidarity with the poor and the oppressed; gratuity as the climate of fruitful work for liberation; joy as victory over suffering; spiritual childhood as a condition of commitment to the poor; and community as a gift born out of the common experience of the dark night of injustice.

This is a very dynamic spirituality that asks for constant, careful listening to the people of God and especially to the poor. It does not allow for a fixed and definitive theory that can be applied at all times and in all places. It requires great attentiveness to the continually new movements of the Spirit among the children of God. That in turn requires an ear that has been well trained by the Scriptures and the church's understanding of those Scriptures. A constant dialogue is necessary between the "old knowing" of Scripture and tradition and the "new knowing" of the concrete, daily life experiences of the people of God. Since in Latin

America that daily life includes the experience of flagrant injustice, political manipulation, and paralyzing corruption, this dialogue often has more the character of a confrontation than of an easy conversation. But only through faithfulness to that dialogue can an authentic, vital, and fruitful spirituality develop.

It is hard to fully grasp the depth of this spirituality. Gustavo summarizes it in St. Paul's words as a teaching that sets us "free to love"—words that describe not only a spirituality of liberation but all Christian spirituality from the desert Fathers to such men and women of our own time as Charles de Foucauld, Dorothy Day, and Thomas Merton. When Gustavo points to this freedom as the goal of a spirituality of liberation, he connects the struggle of the people of Latin America with the spiritual struggle of all the great Christians throughout the centuries. More clearly than before, we can now see that this is the struggle not just of heroic individuals but of the people as a community of faith. It is precisely the new understanding of the church as the people of God that has made this perspective possible and fruitful.

This freedom to love is the freedom to which many Latin Americans dedicate their lives. The great paradox is that we North Americans, who have the word "freedom" written all over our history books, are now being challenged to learn the full meaning of freedom from our oppressed brothers and sisters in the South. In the free world of the United States, where most of the world's wealth is concentrated, spiritual freedom is often hard to find. Many Christians in the North are imprisoned by their fears and guilt. They have more than they need but less freedom than their fellow Christians in Latin America who are struggling hard to survive.

I had direct experience of this paradox during three months in Peru. Although I had gone there hoping to be able to give, I found myself first of all the receiver. The poor with whom I lived revealed to me the treasures of a Christian spirituality that had been hidden from me in my own affluent world. While having little or nothing, they taught me true gratitude. While struggling with unemployment, malnutrition, and many diseases, they taught me joy. While oppressed and exploited, they taught me community. During my short stay among the poor of Peru, I had just a glimpse of that spirituality which Gustavo articulates in such a masterly way. *We Drink from Our Own Wells* is an important book not just because it is an intelligent and insightful presentation of a Latin American spirituality, but more so because it is a gift from the poor that through Gustavo's ministry of solidarity has now become available for the conversion of us who always thought of ourselves as self-sufficient.

By way of conclusion, I would like to speak of a conviction that has been deepened and strengthened by this book. It is the conviction that the spiritual destiny of the people of North America is intimately connected with the spiritual destiny of the people in Latin America. I am increasingly struck by the thought that what is happening in the Christian communities of Latin America is part of God's way of calling us in the North to conversion. I even feel that knowing God in North America can no longer be separated from the way God is making himself known in Latin America.

As we see the increasing violence in Central America, that inflamed cord that binds the two continents together, we must humbly confess that something more than political conflict is happening there. It is a deeply spiritual crisis that involves both Americas, North and South. It is a crisis that reveals the failure of five centuries of Christianity to bring unity to the Americas. The oppression, violence, and mass murder that ravage El Salvador and Guatemala remind us that we are crucifying Christ again. But his death among us is also a "kairos," an opportunity for conversion. In the name of millions of the nameless poor, Gustavo reaches out a hand to us and calls us to open our hearts again to the life-giving Spirit of Christ so that healing and reconciliation may be realized among Christians and the Risen Lord be victorious over the power of death.

—Henri J. M. Nouwen

INTRODUCTION

A Christian is defined as a follower of Jesus, and reflection on the experience of following constitutes the central theme of any solid theology. The experience and the reflection alike have for their subject a community that under the movement of the Spirit focuses its life on the proclamation of the good news: the Lord is risen! Death and injustice are not the final word of history. Christianity is a message of life, a message based on the gratuitous love of the Father for us.

Since the very first days of the theology of liberation, the question of spirituality (specifically: the following of Jesus) has been of deep concern.[1] Moreover, the kind of reflection that the theology of liberation represents is conscious of the fact that it was, and continues to be, preceded by the spiritual experience of Christians who are committed to the process of liberation. That experience is at the heart of the movement set afoot by the poor of Latin America as they seek to assert their human dignity and their status as daughters and sons of God. This reaching out for life situates the place and time of an encounter with the Lord. And this encounter becomes in turn the starting point for a route to be taken in the following of Jesus Christ.[2]

The importance assigned to this experience in the theology of liberation is in keeping with the purpose of that theology, which is to develop a reflection that is concerned with and based on practice in the light of faith. Consequently, in the area of spirituality too the varying conditions and ways of practice will lead to new perspectives and new themes. The breakthrough or irruption—as it has been called[3]—of the poor in Latin America not only left its mark on the beginning of the theology of liberation but is daily becoming more urgent and massive, even where the effort is made to hide or repress it. This has simply reinforced the fact that the

1

entrance of the poor onto center stage in Latin American society and the Latin American church has plowed new furrows for Christian life and reflection.

The furrows are watered at times with the blood of witnesses (martyrs) to that preferential love of God for the poor that is today leaving an indelible imprint on the life of the church in Latin America. This martyrdom is setting a seal on the following of Jesus and the subsequent theological reflection that are now coming into existence in Latin America. Ours is a land of premature and unjust death, but also of an ever stronger assertion of the right to life and to the joy of Easter.

In part 1 of this book I try to say something about the contextual experience that is the matrix or crucible of the spirituality now being born in Latin America. It is a serious historical mistake to reduce what is happening among us today to a social or political problem. Consequently, one shows a lack of Christian insight if one thinks that the challenges to spirituality are simply those raised by the relationship between faith and the political order, by the defense of human rights, or by the struggle for justice.

These problems are, of course, present and call urgently for an adequate response. They do not, however, reveal their full meaning unless they are situated in turn within a broader and deeper problematic—namely, the very one we have attempted to sum up in the word "liberation." Liberation is an all-embracing process that leaves no dimension of human life untouched, because when all is said and done it expresses the saving action of God in history. This understanding is based on the conviction that the poverty being experienced in Latin America (and other parts of the world), along with its causes and consequences, is *death-dealing* and denies the basic human right to existence and the *reign of life*.

The situation is not a simple one, and we must not let ourselves be naive about it. The challenges come from various quarters. Our present situation is beset with difficulties and possibilities; equivocal solutions prompted by despair are offered, but so are lines of action that respect the deepest human values. Incredible self-centeredness and pride of every kind make their appearance, but so do acts of humble and unlimited generosity. Some enthusiasts want to make everything over, while others urge creative undertakings that are marked by sensitivity to the most worth-while traditions of the Latin American peoples.

When an entire world is thus in upheaval, it is impossible not to question the manner in which Latin Americans live their Christianity, and there is need of political and spiritual discernment. We must pay careful heed to these questions if we want to be alert to what the Lord has to say to us in the context of our own history. Within that history new and fruitful paths are opening up that are nonetheless tied into a very rich spiritual tradition. The combination creates a favorable time for recognizing the presence of the God of life and for proclaiming the kingdom of God and its justice.

In part 2 I try to define the main aspects of every spirituality, every following of Jesus. To this end a study of the sacred scriptures is indispensable. Every spirituality receives its initial impulse from an encounter with the Lord. That experience determines the path to be followed; it bears permanently the mark of the divine initiative and of the historical context in which it occurred.

Paul says that the following (imitation) of Jesus is a "walking according to the Spirit" who is life and who enables us to live in freedom. Every experience of following brings home to us the fact that there is no path marked out in advance in its every detail. Rather it is a way that is established in the very going, as Machado puts it in his poetry. Thus, Paul's dispute with the law brings him to the point of boldly asserting the "freedom of the children of God." The law is linked to death, freedom to life. The apostle tells us that we are free to love. This approach sheds light on the process that Latin America is now undergoing. In the final analysis, to liberate is to give life—life in its totality. It is in this framework that distinctions between the material and the spiritual, the temporal and the religious, the personal and the social, and others of the same kind, must be understood (and not suppressed). The study of Paul shows us that in his eyes the basic opposition is between *death* and *life*. The present situation in Latin America is making us newly aware of the great scope of that opposition with respect to our Christian life.

Furthermore, the "walking" is that of an entire people. The Bible in fact depicts it as a collective venture: under the prior action of the God who liberates, a people breaks out of exploitation and death, crosses the desert, and reaches the promised land. Or, if you will, it is the venture of a "messianic people" itself called *the way* in the book that recounts that people's *Acts*. These biblical paradigms have inspired Christian experience and reflection on this theme down through the history of spirituality. They bring home to us the fact that the journey is a community journey and that it is also all-embracing. Spirituality is not concerned simply with a particular area of Christian existence; it is a style of life that puts its seal on our way of accepting the gift of filiation (the basis of fellowship) to which the Father calls us.

The effort to define the main aspects of every spirituality will enable me to outline, in part 3, what is happening today in Latin America. In that part of the world the encounter with the Lord takes specific forms, as does the people's journeying in accordance with the Spirit. It is important to call attention to the characteristics of this particular spiritual experience. My remarks amount simply to a series of rapid and rather rough strokes of the brush in an effort to sketch a profile that even now is only barely emerging. I think, nonetheless, that, as in every following of Jesus, the experiences of commitment to liberation make possible a differentiated reading of some basic gospel themes. They also cause us to be challenged by the ideas of the gospel. My concern here is to bring out the relationship between challenge and historical situation, for from it there will perhaps emerge the characteristic traits of this spirituality that is only now seeing the light of day.

For obvious reasons the only thing I can do is to illustrate this emergent spirituality with texts that express the spiritual experience of Christians in Latin America. Unwritten testimonies and many other texts cannot be cited in this volume, but they are present to my mind; despite the difficulties of the task I wish to be faithful to all these witnesses. Their testimonies have made it possible for me to follow what has been happening over recent years in my own country, Peru, and in all Latin America. It is from the experience of this following that I have sought to write the pages of this book.

One of the main guiding ideas in these pages is the conviction that the historical starting point for the following of Jesus and for reflection on this following is to be found in the experience that comes from the Spirit. This is what Bernard of Clairvaux put so beautifully when he said that when it comes to spirituality all people must know how to "drink from their own well."[4] In our insertion into the process of liberation in which the peoples of Latin America are now engaged, we live out the gift of faith, hope, and charity that makes us disciples of the Lord. This experience is our well. The water that rises out of it continually purifies us and smooths away any wrinkles in our manner of being Christians, at the same time supplying the vital element needed for making new ground fruitful.[5]

PART ONE

How Shall We Sing to the Lord in a Foreign Land?

There is no Christian life without "songs" to the Lord, without thanksgiving for God's love, and without prayer. But the songs are sung by persons living in particular historical situations, and these provide the framework within which they perceive God's presence and also God's absence (in the biblical sense of this term; see Jer. 7:1–7; Matt. 7:15–21). In our Latin American context we may well ask ourselves: How can we thank God for the gift of life when the reality around us is one of premature and unjustly inflicted death? How can we express joy at knowing ourselves to be loved by the Father when we see the suffering of our brothers and sisters? How can we sing when the suffering of an entire people chokes the sound in our throats?

These questions are troublesome and far from superficial; they are not to be stilled by facile answers that underestimate the situation of injustice and marginalization in which the vast majority of

Latin Americans live. On the other hand, it is also evident that this reality does not silence the song or make inaudible the voice of the poor. This state of affairs amounts to a critical judgment on many aspects of the spirituality that is still accepted in some Christian circles. At the same time, however, it represents a "favorable time" (2 Cor. 6:2, JB), a *kairos*, a moment of heightened revelation both of God and of new paths on the journey of fidelity to the word of God.

1

IN A FOREIGN LAND

The situation created by the process of liberation—a process that in its varied embodiments is attacking the age-old wretchedness and exploitation that have characterized Latin America—is raising serious questions about a certain approach to Christian life. It is causing persons to break with that approach and launching them on new quests. Familiar reference points are being obscured; confusion, frustration, and defensive withdrawal are experienced on a wide scale. But a process of reevaluation is also in evidence and new paths are being opened. All this is a judgment being passed by history: a history in this case that the poor and the dispossessed—those who are the privileged ones in God's kingdom—have begun to create. The judgment is thus also one being passed by God. Let me point out some of the more salient aspects of this *krisis* or judgment.

An Alien World

Latin American reality is characterized by a poverty that the Final Puebla Document (PD) describes as "inhuman" (no. 29) and "anti-evangelical" (no. 1151). Such poverty represents a situation of "institutionalized violence," to use the well-known phrase of Medellín ("Peace," no. 16).

The real issue in this situation is becoming increasingly clear to us today: poverty means death. It means death due to hunger and sickness, or to the repressive methods used by those who see their privileged position being endangered by any effort to liberate the oppressed. It means physical death to which is added cultural death, inasmuch as those in power seek to do away with everything that gives unity and strength to the dispossessed of this world. In this way those in power hope to make the dispossessed an easier prey for the machinery of oppression.

Perception of the reality of death penetrating a rural area that has become alien is well expressed in a heart-rending letter that came from Haiti, the poorest country in Latin America. Faced with the threat of the eviction of rural populations because of a government project, a group of Christians writes:

> These fields are our entire life, our entire support. They give us food. Thanks to them we can send our children to school. . . . Farmhands can no longer find work, even as day laborers. How are we to live? . . . Where can we go? If we move to Port-au-Prince our situation will only be worse, because there is such misery there. If we go to the mountains, what kind of land can we expect to till? Must we, then, leave Haiti—get on a boat in order to discover the misery in other places? We do not deserve this torture.[1]

The conclusion bespeaks a bitter realism: "Wherever we look, we see death."

It is this that is really meant when we talk of poverty and of the destruction of individuals and peoples, cultures and traditions. In particular, it is what is meant when we speak of the poverty of those most dispossessed: Amerindians and Latin American blacks, and the women of these doubly marginalized and oppressed sectors of the population. Consequently, despite what is sometimes thought, we are not dealing here simply with a "social situation," as though it were a state of affairs unrelated to the fundamental demands of the gospel message. Rather we are confronted with a reality contrary to the reign of life that the Lord proclaims.

In the Bible the land is one object of the promise of life. The children of God are promised a land of their own in which they will live as the proper inhabitants and not as outsiders or strangers. A foreign land, on the contrary, is a place of injustice and death (for the Jewish people the prototypes of such a land were, first, Egypt and, later on, Babylon, as in Psalm 137 from which I have taken the title of the present chapter). A "foreign" land is one that is hostile and has therefore lost its meaning as a gift from God.

Age-old oppression, intensified by the repressive measures with which the powerful seek to hinder all social change,[2] creates a situation in which the vast Latin American majorities are dispossessed and therefore compelled to live as strangers in their own land.[3] For this reason, the breakthrough of the poor into Latin American history and the Latin American church is based on a new and profound grasp of this experience of estrangement. The exploited and marginalized are today becoming increasingly conscious of living in a foreign land that is hostile to them, a land of death, a land that has no concern for their most legitimate interests and serves only as a tool for their oppressors, a land that is alien to their hopes and is owned by those who seek to terrorize them.[4]

This experience has historical roots in the vision of the sixteenth-century Amerindians of Peru: their land had become a foreign territory, a world turned inside out by the European conquerors. The situation therefore called for a radical change, a cosmic cataclysm (*pachacuti* is the Quechuan term), that would put the universe back on its feet by establishing a just order.[5]

Exiled, therefore, by unjust social structures from a land that in the final analysis belongs to God alone—"all the earth is mine" (Exod. 19:5, JB; cf. Deut. 10:14)—but aware now that they have been despoiled of it, the poor are actively entering into Latin American history and are taking part in an exodus that will restore to them what is rightfully their own. This struggle for their rights is located within a quest for the kingdom of God and its justice—in other words, the struggle is part of a journey to a meeting with the God of the kingdom. It is a collective undertaking of liberation in which the classic spiritual combat is making more searching demands because it has taken on social and historical dimensions.[6]

The result is that those who involve themselves in this struggle likewise become "strangers" to Latin American society and even to some sectors of the church.[7] They are in fact alienated from the status quo and its beneficiaries, who regard themselves as the owners of lands, goods, and persons.[8] In these circumstances, efforts to change the situation can come only from "outside." For (according to the privileged) the Latin American poor are content with their lot; they cherish only the hope of receiving something when they extend their hands and beg, and they thank their generous benefactors for such kindness. And, paradoxically, at bottom the powerful of Latin America are right: the tenacious determination that things must change comes in fact from a land that the powerful have turned into a foreign land for the poverty-stricken masses.

Given these circumstances, it is no surprise that Latin America is today living in an age of suspicion. To those in control every action aiming at liberation and the recovery for the people of what belongs to it, all talk that openly starts with the realization of alienation, is subversive and calls for punishment by the political, military, or ideological authority in the hands of the ruling class. The present situation—which the exploited have now begun to challenge—has been so completely accepted by some and so completely taken to be the proper order of things that every expression of disagreement becomes unnatural and is grounds for suspicion; this holds true even in certain sectors of the church.

At the present time, then, men and women who try to side with the dispossessed and bear witness to God in Latin America must accept the bitter fact that they will inevitably be suspect. They may even be regarded not as followers of Jesus Christ but as intruders: they come from outside, make their way in, and create problems, simply because they think—and, be it said, live— differently. It is hard for them to accept suspicion for something that is so deeply a part of them as their personal honesty and, above all, their faith in the Lord. Such suspicion is an attack on what the old morality used to call a person's "honor," which is a basic right of every person. But honor of this kind can bring persecution, imprisonment, or death. Archbishop Oscar Romero[9] was an example of someone suspected of not being a good Christian. Some of those who entertain such suspicions are simply fearful of the future to which the Lord is calling us. Suspicion within the Christian community itself is nowadays a component of the cross of Christians who seek to bear witness to the God of the poor. By that very fact, it is also a factor that serves to purify their commitment.

Questions

Serious questioners are today challenging the spirituality that until not too long ago was generally accepted in ecclesial circles.[10] I want to single out two characteristics of that spirituality, along with the criticisms now raised against them.

1) Christian spirituality has long been presented as *geared to minorities*. It seems to be the peculiar possession of select and, to some extent, closed groups; it is linked for the most part to the existence of religious orders and congregations. Religious life, in the narrow sense of this term, encompassed a "state of perfection"; it implicitly supposed, therefore, that there were other, imperfect states of Christian life.[11] Religious life was marked by a full and structured quest for holiness; in the other states there were found, at best, only the less demanding elements of this spirituality. The way proper to religious life supposed some kind of separation from the world and its everyday activities (one form of the well-known *fuga mundi*, "flight from the world"). The second way did not call for that kind of effort and could be traveled without fanfare in the midst of occupations that had little or nothing religious about them.

The "spirituality of the laity" that accompanied the rise of the lay apostolic movements in the first decades of our century was a reaction against that perfect/imperfect outlook. It was a reaction at least against its more rigid aspects, those that represented a narrowing and impoverishment of Christian life.[12] The counterclaim was provocative but inadequate, because the spirituality of the laity was still—and could not help being—strongly characterized by important elements taken from the way of Christian perfection that had been canonized by the experience of monastic and religious life.[13]

In reality, though this was not always explicitly recognized or perhaps even desired in every case, that approach implied a distinction that resulted in two classes of Christians or, if you prefer, two ways of Christian life. The distinction was already admitted in the theological schools of earlier centuries and has continued to reappear throughout the history of the church. It is with us, although in more subtle forms, even today.

One thing is certain: any spirituality limited to minorities is today under heavy crossfire. It is challenged on the one side by the spiritual experience of the dispossessed and marginalized—and those who side with them—in their commitment to the struggle for liberation. Out of this experience has come the inspiration for a popular and community quest of the Lord that is incompatible with elitist models. It is challenged, on the other side, by the questioning of those who live a life focused on concerns of the spiritual order and who are now beginning to realize that such a life is made possible for them, at least in part, by their freedom from material worries (food, lodging, health needs).[14] These, of course, are concerns that fill the daily lives of the poor masses of the human race.[15]

It is rather difficult to face up to the fact that the minorities to whom this spirituality is directed are also privileged minorities from the social, cultural, and, to some extent, economic standpoint. In any case, we are dealing here with a matter that calls for radical treatment: a return to the sources, a salvaging of the values contained therein, and a rejection of the inertia and sense of established position that inevitably mark such a situation. Only thus is it possible to prevent the cancerous growth of aspects of spirituality that are legitimate in themselves.

2) A second characteristic of the spirituality in question, and one that is also being challenged today, is its *individualistic bent*.

The spiritual journey has often been presented as a cultivation of individualistic values as a way to personal perfection. The relationship with God seemed to obscure the presence of others and encouraged individual Christians to be absorbed in their own interiority in order to understand and develop it better. For this reason the spiritual life was called *the interior life*,[16] which many understood as a life lived exclusively within the individual. The important thing in it was the deployment of the virtues as potentialities that had to do with the individual and had little or no connection with the outside world. In this outlook the important thing is one's intention. It is this that gives value to human actions; the external effects of these actions are less important. Actions without any apparent human significance thus acquired spiritual and sanctifying value if done for important and legitimate motives.

When only a few authentic dimensions of Christian life are thus developed, the result may be a dangerous privatization of spirituality.[17] As certain spiritual traditions moved away from their sources, they began to flow in the limited channels of the manuals and the spiritual treatises until finally they went astray—and in the process began to dry up—as increasingly shallow streams representing only an individualistic outlook. The community dimensions inherent in all Christian life became formalities; they were unable to alter the perspective that turned the journey to God into a purely individual venture. It is not surprising, then, that in such a context charity should be regarded as simply another Christian virtue to be cultivated.[18]

This manner of understanding the following of Jesus is usually characterized as "spiritualist." The name is based on the fact that it shows little interest in temporal tasks and a great deal of insensitivity to the presence and needs of the real, concrete persons who surround Christians as they follow this spiritual way.

It seems to me that an important source of the "spirituality of evasion," as Puebla calls it (no. 826), is the individualism of which I have been speaking. Individualism operates, in fact, as a filter that makes it possible to "spiritualize" and even volatilize what in the Bible are nuanced statements of a social and historical nature. For example, the poor/rich opposition (a social fact) is reduced to the humble/proud opposition (something within the individual). "Passage" through the individual interiorizes, and robs of their historical bite, categories reflective of the objective realities in which individuals and peoples live and die, struggle and assert their faith.[19] This kind of reduction has often taken place. It is a frequent occurrence in the interpretation of the Magnificat—that profoundly beautiful expression of the spirituality of the poor of Yahweh—when the exegete loses sight of its roots in the life and hopes of Mary's people and, in the final analysis, in the personal experience of the mother of Jesus herself.

Individualism and spiritualism thus combine to impoverish and even distort the following of Jesus. An individualistic spirituality is incapable of offering guidance in this following to those who have embarked on a collective enterprise of liberation. Nor does it do justice to the different dimensions of the human person, including the so-called material aspects that I shall discuss in part 3.[20]

I wanted to bring out these two characteristics of the "traditional" spiritual outlook because they represent what many Christians have experienced and experience still. Individualism and limitation to a minority have led to a distortion of valid spiritual intuitions and experiences. They are being criticized today not only in the light of contemporary experience but also in the light of what emerges from a return to the sources of the intuitions in question. Minority status and individualism are also big with consequences; I shall come back to some of these later on.

New Wine in Old Bottles

The experience of Christians in contemporary Latin America is so new and so harsh that it compels a radical questioning of the kind of spirituality I have been discussing. That is certainly the feeling of everyone who seeks to be in solidarity with the victims of despoliation and poverty. They are indeed victims. That is a point that must be emphasized, for by dint of much talking about the poor and about commitment to them, about their human and Christian values, and about their potential as evangelizers and their other qualities and abilities, we run the risk of forgetting all that is inhuman and anti-evangelical in the situation of poverty. I am talking about the real poverty in which vast majorities of human beings live, and not about the idealized poverty that we sometimes excogitate for our own pastoral, theological, and spiritual purposes.

The harsh reality of everyday experience causes breaks with the past and launches persons on new quests.

1) To the measure that solidarity with the world of the poor grows and matures, old securities collapse and fixed reference points crumble away—underpinnings that used to provide a certain tranquility in the midst of new experiences and challenges. A growing *insecurity* seems to undermine, from within, the patterns of spiritual life that guided our earlier steps. Many continued in

their original commitment for a long time, relying on the solid protection of their religious community, a Christian environment, and a particular way of understanding life according to the gospel. The shock of reality, and the effort to enter into it to an ever fuller degree, darkened what was once a clear horizon. Familiar paths now lead to impasses. Those who, nonetheless, refuse to be discouraged seek more fruitful paths, but the price they pay is dissatisfaction, fear, and sometimes even frustration. And in every case there is a keen sense of insecurity that is perhaps inevitable but that also must pass because it is not possible to build a solid and lasting spirituality on a sense of insecurity.

2) The result is a painful *split* in spiritual experience. Persons begin to live in a somewhat dichotomized fashion. On the one hand, they feel the need of a sure spiritual way; this is especially the case perhaps in those who have had a more systematic formation in this area. On the other hand, daily life with its demands for commitment seems to run on a tangential track; it does not initially conflict with the spirituality one has acquired, but neither does it enrich it. In the long run, this kind of dual existence is highly unsatisfactory. Upon the disappearance of the fixed points that should give unity to everyday activity, persons live at the mercy of events, unable to establish fruitful links between them and forced simply to jump from one to another. They are convinced that they have learned a great deal from solidarity with the poor and from carrying out their work of evangelization among them, but when they try to express this perception they fall back on categories that begin to seem increasingly alien and remote. The problem results from the fact that they have not reexamined these categories in the light of their new experiences or, more exactly, that they do not have another path that can replace the one that no longer seems to lead to the goal.

An important and painful example of the lack of vital unity (which every spirituality demands) is the separation that takes place, beneath all the resplendent phrases, between prayer and action. Both are accepted as necessary, and in fact they are. The problem is to establish a connection between them.[21] Good-will solutions ("everything is prayer"; "I pray with the people") do not eliminate the problem.

Those who find themselves in this predicament grieve, more or less explicitly, for the lost unity of their lives. Many Christians feel inclined, in one or another way, to say with the psalmist:

> Recalling other times I pour out my soul:
>   how I entered the sanctuary and prostrated
>   myself toward the altar,
>   amid songs of joy and thanksgiving
>   amid the bustle of the feast
>   [Ps. 42:5, author's version].

But unity is not to be recovered by eliminating one of the two poles that are in tension. The recovery must rather be—let me repeat—the result of an effort to be faithful, in both prayer and concrete commitments, to the will of the Lord in the midst of the poor. An authentic unity is based on a synthesis of elements that are seemingly disparate but that in fact enrich one another. And the possibilities of such a synthesis emerge in the very midst of the questioning directed at a particular kind of spirituality, in the very midst of the crisis I have tried to describe. The new situation reveals paths to be followed that are the hope-filled opposite of those problematic ones mentioned above.

2

THE SONG OF THE POOR ·

What we are confronted with, then, is a foreign land, a passage through a desert; testing and discernment. But in this same land, from which God is not in fact absent, the seeds of a new spirituality can germinate. This spirituality gives rise to new songs to the Lord, songs filled with an authentic joy because it is spirituality that is nourished by the hope of a people familiar with the suffering caused by poverty and contempt.

The present experience of Latin American Christians is one that has been given profound expression in the psalms. Trusting as he does in the Lord who is "a stronghold for the oppressed" (Ps. 9:9), the psalmist is able to proclaim:

> I will give thanks to the Lord with my whole heart;
> I will tell of all thy wonderful deeds.
> I will be glad and exult in thee,
> I will sing praise to thy name, O Most High
> [Ps. 9:1–2].

Because he is sure that the Lord "loves righteousness and justice" (Ps. 33:5), the psalmist can sing:

> Rejoice in the Lord, O you righteous!
> Praise befits the upright.

> Praise the Lord with the lyre,
>> make melody to him with the harp of ten strings!
> Sing to him a new song,
>> play skillfully on the strings, with loud shouts
>>> [Ps. 33:1–3].

We are living in a favorable time, a *kairos,* in which the Lord says: "Behold, I stand at the door and knock; if any one hears my voice and opens the door, I will come in to him and eat with him, and he with me" (Rev. 3:20). Not a violent entrance but a quiet knock that calls for an attitude of welcome and active watchfulness, of confidence and courage. Indifference, the privileges they have gained, and fear of the new make many persons spiritually deaf; as a result, the Lord passes by without stopping at their houses. But there are also many in our countries and in these times who hear the Lord's call and try to open the doors of their lives. We are living in a special period of God's saving action, a time when a new route is being carved out for the following of Jesus.

A Favorable Time

Our increasingly clear awareness of the harsh situation in Latin America and the sufferings of the poor must not make us overlook the fact that the harshness and suffering are not what is truly new in the present age.[1] What is new is not wretchedness and repression and premature death, for these, unfortunately, are ancient realities in these countries. What is new is that the people are beginning to grasp the causes of their situation of injustice and are seeking to release themselves from it. Likewise new and important is the role which faith in the God who liberates is playing in the process.

It can therefore be said without any fear of exaggeration that we are experiencing today an exceptional time in the history of Latin America and the life of the church. Of this situation we may say with Paul: "Now is the favorable time; this is the day of salvation" (2 Cor. 6:2, JB). Such a vision of things does not make the journey of the poor less difficult nor does it gloss over the obstacles they encounter in their efforts to defend their most elementary rights. The demanding, cruel reality of wretchedness, exploitation, hostility, and death—our daily experience—will not allow us to forget it. There is question here, then, not of a facile optimism but rather of a deep trust in the historical power of the poor and, above all, a firm hope in the Lord.

These attitudes do not automatically ensure a better future; but as they draw nourishment from a present that is full of possibilities, they in turn nourish the present with promises. So true is this that if we do not respond to the demands of the present, because we do not know in advance whither we may be led, we are simply refusing to hear the call of Jesus Christ. We are refusing to open to him when he knocks on the door and invites us to sup with him.

We are today experiencing a *time of solidarity* in Latin America. Throughout its length and breadth there is a growing movement of solidarity in defense of human rights and, in particular, the rights of the poor. This has been true of Nicaragua, El Salvador, Guatemala, and Bolivia; it is true also of those who have been exiled or have disappeared in Haiti, Uruguay, Chile, Argentina, Paraguay, and other countries. More than this, at the base level and the local level there has been a proliferation of groups and organizations dedicated to solidarity among and with the dispossessed.[2] The ease with which the popular sectors move from the local scene to the Latin American scene is impressive. This is the first flowering at the continental level of what José María Arguedas used to call "the fellowship of the wretched."[3] The anonymous heroes involved in these efforts are countless, and the generosity poured out in them is beyond measure.

Recent events in European history have made the word "solidarity" fashionable. In the Latin American experience, however, for many years now the word has been used among the poor of the continent for the action that follows upon their new awareness of their situation of exploitation and marginalization, as well as of the role they must play in the building of a new and different society. For Christians this action is an efficacious act of charity, of love for neighbor and love for God in the poor. Christians thus realize that the question is not simply one of personal attitudes. The issue is the solidarity of the entire ecclesial community— the church—with movements of the poor in defense of their rights.

This accounts for the rise of many groups whose purpose is not simply to practice solidarity themselves but also to help the church as a whole to bear witness to, and to live up to, its proclamation of the reign of God.[4]

The present is also a *time of prayer*. Anyone who is in contact with base-level ecclesial communities can attest that there is a great deal of intense and hope-filled prayer going on in Latin America today. Yet the forecasters of doom and failure, those of the type whom at the beginning of the Second Vatican Council John XXIII spoke of as "prophets of gloom," have been claiming that the life of prayer is vanishing from Latin America.

Latin Americans at the base level have a completely different experience. Nor am I speaking only of those great moments that are milestones in the journey of a people with its advances and retreats. At such moments the communities have given evidence of great creativity and depth in the matter of prayer. But when I speak of the wealth and intensity of prayer I have in mind also, and above all, the daily practice of humble prayer in numberless localities. Nowhere in the Latin American church is more fervent and joyous prayer to be found amid daily suffering and struggle than in the Christian communities among the poor. It is our acts of gratitude and hope in the Lord that make us free (Gal. 5:1).

For many, then (I am indeed not unaware of the failures of some in this area), a growing maturity in their solidarity with the commitment to liberation has, by a dialectical process, brought with it a new emphasis on prayer as a fundamental dimension of Christian life. The result has been a mighty development of prayer in popular Christian groups. I know how difficult it is to measure such things, but daily experience, and even the result in writings (this among a people for whom oral expression is the dominant kind), are proof that prayer is widespread and creative.

It is, then, a time of solidarity and a time of prayer—but also, and in a sense synthesizing those two, a *time of martyrdom* as well. There are many who have devoted their lives, to the point of suffering death, in order to bear witness to the presence of the poor in the Latin American world and to the preferential love that God has for them.[5] Nor has the bloodletting ceased as yet. The first manifestations of this unparalleled and astonishing situation (after all, when many of the persecutors and murderers come out into the open, they claim to be Christians)[6] go back to about 1968.[7] We are perhaps still too close historically to these events to be able to gauge their full significance.

What did the contemporaries of the early martyrs think about the events of their time? Perhaps the complexity of the factors in any historical situation, their own closeness to the events, and even their lack of personal courage prevented them from seeing the significance of occurrences that today seem so clearly to have been heroic testimonies to faith in the Lord. It is a fact that a consensus with regard to what is happening before our eyes is always more difficult to reach; this is because present events, unlike those of the past, are not situated in a world that we regard as idyllic and that we envelop in golden legends. Present events form part of our own universe and demand of the individual a personal decision, a rejection of every kind of complicity with executioners, a straightforward solidarity, an uncompromising denunciation of evil, a prayer of commitment.

But the poor are not fooled; they see the truth and speak out when others remain silent.[8] They see in the surrender of these lives a profound and radical testimony of faith; they observe that in a continent where the powerful spread death in order to protect their privileges, such a testimony to God often brings the murder of the witness; and they draw nourishment from the hope that sustains these lives and these deaths. According to the very earliest Christian tradition the blood of martyrs gives life to the ecclesial community, the assembly of the disciples of Jesus Christ. This is what is happening today in Latin America. Fidelity unto death is a wellspring of life. It signals a new, demanding, and fruitful course in the following of Jesus.[9]

The new way is, of course, not entirely new. The present-day Latin American experience of martyrdom bids us all turn back to one of the major sources of all spirituality: the blood-stained experience of the early Christian community, which was so weak in the face of the imperial power of that day.[10]

I have spoken of questions and crises. These two terms, however, do not adequately cover the total reality of the following of Jesus in present-day Latin America; in fact, they are not even most representative of that following. They simply represent a road that must be traveled and a price that must be paid for the sake of what is fundamental: *the recognition of the time of salvation* in which these countries are now living. A little earlier I cited Psalm 42. But, despite the words I quoted, the psalmist's prayer is not turned nostalgically to the past, for such nostalgia would mean attachment to our own feelings rather than to God. The psalmist in fact goes on to say:

> Why are you cast down, O my soul,
>   and why are you disquieted within me?
> Hope in God; for I shall again praise him,
>   my help and my God. . . .
> Oh send out thy light and thy truth;
>   let them lead me,
> let them bring me to thy holy hill
>   and to thy dwelling!
> Then I will go to the altar of God,
>   to God my exceeding joy;
> and I will praise thee with the lyre,
>   O God, my God [Ps. 42:11; 43:3–4].

The "I shall again give him praise" is already a present reality. The Latin American church is passing through an unparalleled period of its history. The concrete and efficacious commitment of so many Christians to the poorest and most disinherited, as well as the serious difficulties they encounter in their commitment to solidarity, are leaving a profound mark on the history of Latin America.[11] The attitude of those who believe they can continue to rely on the support of the church for maintaining their privileges is changing, but so is the attitude of those who were beginning to look upon the church as an institution belonging to the past. We are not now in the evening of the history of the church but are beginning the new day of an opportunity for evangelization that we never had before.

To some all this may smack of facile and naive optimism. True enough, the exhaustion produced by an unending situation of wretchedness; the tensions caused by the resistance men and women must engage in if they are to win out in their commitment to liberation; the depression felt at the abiding attitude of suspicion that greets every effort at effective solidarity with an exploited people; the resistance experienced within the people of God itself—these facts do not permit an easy optimism or allow us to forget the marginalization, the suffering, the deaths. At the same time, however, we must be aware of the change that has taken place. When all is said and done, despite—or thanks to—the immense price that is being paid, the present situation is nourishing new life, revealing new paths to be followed, and providing reason for profound joy.

The spendthrift generosity (sometimes accompanied by the giver's own blood, as I have pointed out) that has been shown in Latin America in recent years is making its nations fruitful and is confronting the ecclesial community with a demanding, but at the same time, most promising moment in its history. In the faces and hands of the dispossessed the Lord is knocking, and knocking loudly, on the community's door. By feeding the hope of the poor (that is what Archbishop Romero accepted as his pastoral mission)[12] the church will be accepting the banquet to which the Lord of the kingdom invites us. Two paragraphs above, I mentioned "an opportunity for evangelization." The question is, Do we know how to make use of that opportunity?

Solidarity, prayer, and martyrdom add up to a time of salvation and judgment, a time of grace and stern demand—a time, above all, of hope.

Toward a New Spirituality

The period that Latin America is now living through is filled with questions and varied perspectives, with impasses and new pathways, with suffering and hope. For this reason it is also becoming the crucible in which a new and different way of following Jesus is being developed. "Different" means proper to Latin America and shaped by the real experiences of the Latin American countries.

In these countries the pain that is felt at the wretchedness of the poor and the atrocities to which they are subjected, but also the love of God that burns especially in those who have given their lives out of love for their brothers and sisters, have become a fire that consumes—and fuses—the disparate elements of our Latin

American reality and our Latin American history. From this action—which is only apparently destructive, inasmuch as in it a basically creative work is also being accomplished—there is emerging the "gold refined by fire" (Rev. 3:18) of a new spirituality. If we reject what is presently occurring and if we are not even willing to be thus consumed, along with our weapons and our baggage, we remain bogged down in what is secondary and anecdotal and perhaps even in the deformity and perversity that marks what is happening in Latin America today. We prefer a selfish inertia to constancy, illusion to hope, the honor of worldly trappings to a profound fidelity to the church, fads to the truly new, authoritarianism to moral authority and service, a tranquilizing past to a challenging present. In short, we prefer mammon to the God of Jesus Christ.

Historical Movements and the Following of Jesus

Every great spirituality is connected with the great historical movement of the age in which it was formulated. This linkage is not to be understood in the sense of mechanical dependence, but the following of Jesus is something that penetrates deeply into the course of human history. This is true, for example, of the mendicant spirituality that was born at a time when, despite apparent good health, the first germs of a crisis for Christianity were incubating. The new spiritual way was closely linked to those movements of the poor that represented a social and evangelical reaction to the wealth and power that the church had attained at that time.[13] The time of the pontificate of Innocent III (1198–1216) showed clearly the heights that the political power and affluence of the church had reached. Without attention to the historical context in which Francis of Assisi and Dominic Guzmán developed their apostolate and bore their evangelical witness, it is impossible to understand either the full significance of the mendicant orders or the reception and resistance they encountered.[14]

The same holds true for Ignatius of Loyola. His spirituality had for its context the transition to the so-called modern age. The broadening of the known world by geographical discoveries, the assertion of human reason that found expression in the birth of experimental science, the extension of the scope of human subjectivity in religious matters as evidenced by the Protestant Reformation—these were converging phenomena that led to a new way of understanding the role of human freedom. It was not a mere coincidence that freedom, a freedom directed to the service of God and others, should be a central theme in Ignatian spirituality.

Examples might be multiplied (John of the Cross and Teresa of Avila and their relationship to the reform within the Catholic Church, and many others). They would only confirm what I have already said: the concrete forms of the following of Jesus are connected with the great historical movements of an age.

A grasp of that constant enables us to understand what is happening before our eyes today in Latin America. Perhaps we lack the perspective required for realizing what is happening, inasmuch as the immediacy of events makes impossible the distance needed. The events are there, nonetheless, and we have begun to experience the change. The breakthrough of the poor to which I referred at the beginning of part 1 is finding expression in the consciousness of the identity and the organization of the oppressed and marginalized of Latin America. In the future, Latin American society will be judged, and transformed, in terms of the poor. These are the ones who in this foreign land of death that is Latin America seek what G. García Márquez, in his beautiful address upon receiving the Nobel Prize, called the utopia of life: "Faced with oppression, pillage, and abandonment, our response is life. . . . It is a new and splendid utopia of life, where no one can decide for others how they will die, where love will be certain and happiness possible, and where those condemned to a hundred years of solitary confinement find, finally and forever, a second chance on this earth."[15]

In search of this utopia, an entire people—with all its traditional values and the wealth of its recent experience—has taken to the path of building a world in which persons are more important than things and in which all can live with dignity, a society that respects human freedom when it is in the service of a genuine common good, and exercises no kind of coercion, from whatever source.

All this we call the historical process of liberation, and with its ideas and its impetuosity it is sweeping all Latin America. The process is only beginning. It is not advancing triumphantly and without obstacles to the applause of the entire world; it is not reaching into all the corners of the Latin American landscape or all the nooks and crannies of the lives of those who live there. Nonethless we are in the presence of a coherent and dynamic movement that is bringing out what is best and most promising in the peoples of Latin America.

Nor is the movement principally a movement within the church; it is rather something that is happening in the history of the Latin American peoples as a whole. For that very reason, however, the movement involves, and is reflected in, the church. The movement is a far-reaching one that is leaving its inescapable mark on the world in which the church lives and in which it must be a sacrament of salvation and a community of witnesses to the life of the risen Christ.

The struggles of the poor for liberation represent an assertion of their right to life. The poverty that the poor suffer means death: a premature and unjust death. It is on the basis of this affirmation of life that the poor of Latin America are trying to live their faith, recognize the love of God, and proclaim their hope. Within these struggles, with their many forms and phases, an oppressed and believing people is increasingly creating a way of Christian life, a spirituality. Latin American Christians will thus cease to be consumers of spiritualities that are doubtless valid but that nonetheless reflect other experiences and other goals, for they are carving out their own way of being faithful both to the Lord and to the experiences of the poorest.

This historical movement, with its focus in the process of liberation, is truly the terrain on which a people's spiritual experience is located as it affirms its right to life. This is the soil in which its response to the gift of faith in the God of life is taking root. The poverty that brings death to the poor is no longer a motive for resignation to the conditions of present existence, nor does it discourage Latin American Christians in their aspirations. The historical experience of liberation that they are now beginning to have is showing them, or reminding them of, something down deep in themselves: that God wants them to live.

A reading in the light of faith, then, gives us to understand that the breakthrough of the poor in Latin American society and the Latin American church is in the final analysis a breakthrough of God in our lives. This breakthrough is the point of departure and also the axis of the new spirituality. It therefore points out to us the way that leads to the God of Jesus Christ.

Choose Life and You Shall Live (Deut. 30:19)

It may seem somewhat reckless to speak of a spirituality taking shape amid the Latin American poor, but that is precisely what is happening as I see it. Perhaps some are surprised because they think of the struggle for liberation as taking place in the social and political sphere, and thus in an area that had nothing to do with the spiritual. Clearly, everything depends here on what one understands by "spiritual." I shall have occasion further on to define this term more closely; for the moment, let me say that the process of liberation is a global one and that it affects every dimension of the human.[16] Moreover, the poverty in which the vast majority of Latin Americans live is not simply a "social problem"; it is a human situation that issues a profound challenge to the Christian conscience.

Surprise may also come from the idea that the subject of the experience that is giving rise to a spirituality is an entire people, and not an individual who stands apart and is to some extent isolated, at least initially. This is another point I must discuss more fully. What is happening among us today represents a departure from the beaten path; it also forces us to realize that the following of Jesus is not along a private route but is part of a collective enterprise. In this way we recover the biblical understanding of people's journey in search of God.

The spirituality being born in Latin America is the spirituality of the church of the poor, to which Pope John XXIII called all of us, the spirituality of an ecclesial community that is trying to make effective its solidarity with the poorest of this world. It is a collective, ecclesial spirituality that, without losing anything of its universal perspective, is stamped with the religious outlook of an exploited and believing people. The journey is one undertaken by the entire people of God. It leaves behind it a land of oppression and, without illusions but with constancy, seeks its way in the midst of a desert. It is a "new" spirituality because the love of the Lord who urges us to reject inertia and inspires us to creativity is itself always new.

In this following of Jesus the central drama is played out in the dialectic of *death followed by life*. In this dialectic and in the victory of the risen Jesus, the God of our hope is revealed. This is a profound and strictly paschal spirituality. It bears in mind all the things that exploit and marginalize the poor, and it draws its nourishment from the victory against the "death out of due time" (as Bartolomé de Las Casas put it) that that situation entails. It embodies the conviction that life, not death, has the final word. The following of Jesus feeds upon the witness given by the resurrection, which means the death of death, and upon the liberating efforts of the poor to assert their unquestionable right to life.[17]

The relationship between an oppressive system and the God who liberates, between death that seems to have the upper hand and the God of life, adumbrates a way of following Jesus and being his disciples under the conditions now prevailing in Latin America. Jesus is not to be sought among the dead: he is alive (Luke 24:5). To seek him among the living is to choose life, as the Book of Deuteronomy says. This choice is the basis of a spiritual experience that is pointing the way to a new path in the following of Jesus in Latin America.[18]

Making Our Own the Spiritual Experience of the People

For many Latin American Christians at the present time the possibility of following Jesus depends on their ability to make their own the spiritual experience of the poor. This requires of them a deep-going conversion; they are being asked to make their own the experience that the poor have of God and of God's will that every human being have life.

In the past, Christians, formed in one or another spiritual school—missionaries, for example—may have felt that it was for them to communicate their own experiences to the people and to point out to the people the path of a suitable Christian life. Today, however, they are called upon to turn that past attitude around. The "evangelizing potential" that Puebla (no. 1147) recognizes in the poor and oppressed points implicitly to one source of that power and ability to proclaim the Chrisitan message. That source is precisely the spiritual experience to which the revelation of God's preference for "mere children" (cf. Matt. 11:25) gives rise. It is this encounter with the Lord that the Christians I am speaking of must make their own.

The need is not simply to recognize that the experience of the people raises questions and challenges for the spirituality of these Christians. That may have been the case for a time. Many of those bound by religious vows, for example, have felt challenged by the real poverty of the dispossessed and marginalized. They asked themselves what meaning their own promise of living a poor life had in the face of such a situation. The questions were legitimate ones and showed a sensitivity entirely deserving of respect. At present, however, the situation is a more inclusive one and reaches deeper. We are no longer faced with isolated questions, however penetrating. Something more systematic is making its appearance; its parts resist separation: they form an organic whole. In this framework the religious vows are recovering their full meaning.

This new reality invites Christians to leave the familiar world they have long inhabited, and leads many of them to reread their own spiritual tradition. Above all, it is a question of making our own the world of the poor and their manner of living out their relationship with the Lord and taking over the historical practice of Jesus.[19] Otherwise we shall be traveling a road that simply parallels that taken by oppressed believers. Then we shall have to try to build bridges that connect these different roads: bridges of commitment to the exploited, friendly relationships with some of them, celebration of the Eucharist with them, and so on. All these would be meritorious efforts no doubt, but they are inadequate because such connections do not change the fact that the roads are only parallel. At the present time, the spiritual experience of the poor is too radical and too comprehensive in scope to merit only that kind of attention. That is why I have spoken here of making that experience our own. That is the issue. Any other response will be a halfway response.

For those who are located within a particular spiritual tradition, entry into the experience of the poor means taking that tradition with them. A rich variety has marked the ways in which throughout its history the Christian community has undertaken the following of Jesus; these ways represent experiences that we cannot simply leave behind. Advantage must rather be taken of that tradition in order to enrich the contemporary spiritual experience of the poor. The refusal thus to enrich the poor would betray a kind of avarice in the area of spirituality. Furthermore, such avarice turns against the distrustful owners: their spiritual riches spoil and lose their value when kept "under the mattress." It is appropriate here to recall the parable of the buried talents.

The faith and hope in the God of life that provide a shelter in the situation of death and struggle for life in which the poor and oppressed of Latin America are now living—they are the well from which we must drink if we want to be faithful to Jesus. This is the water of which Archbishop Oscar Romero had drunk when he said he had been converted to Christ by his own people.[20] Once this change had taken place, he could not but view his following of Jesus as closely bound up with the life (and death) of the Salvadoran people whose sufferings and hopes we all carry in our hearts. His spiritual life abandoned the ways of individualism and began instead to draw its nourishment from the experiences of an entire people. This is why he could say two weeks before he was murdered:

> My life has been threatened many times. I have to confess that, as a Christian, I don't believe in death without resurrection. If they kill me, *I will rise again in the Salvadoran people.* I'm not boasting, or saying this out of pride, but rather as humbly as I can.[21]

We all have the same vocation: to rise to life with the people in its spirituality. This implies a death to the alleged "spiritual ways" that individualisms of one or another kind create but that in fact lead only to an impasse. It also supposes a birth into new ways of being disciples of Jesus, the risen Christ. The newness draws its strength from the Bible and from the best in the history of spirituality and in this respect is profoundly traditional. Such is the experience of the poor of Latin America. Theirs is an authentic spiritual experience, an encounter with the Lord who points out a road for them to follow.

In part 3 I intend to sketch some markings of this itinerary. But first it is necessary to examine what can be called the "dimensions" of a full spirituality—dimensions that are also those of the spiritual path that is being opened up in Latin America.

PART TWO

Here There Is No Longer Any Way

The following of Jesus is a central theme in the New Testament, where its basic characteristics are examined from various angles. If we for our part are to determine the meaning of a "spirituality," we must turn first of all to the scriptural sources, but without on that account neglecting the dialogue with spiritual tradition.

Discipleship is rooted in the experience of an encounter with Jesus Christ. It is an encounter of friends ("No longer do I call you servants . . . but I have called you friends": John 15:15) in which the Lord takes the initiative, and it is the point of departure for a journey. St. Paul speaks of this journey as "a walking according to the Spirit" (Rom. 8:4). And in fact the search for God is a walking in freedom. John of the Cross emphasizes this "walking in freedom" in his *Ascent of Mount Carmel* and, toward the middle of that ascent, explains: "Here there is no longer any way, because for the just man there is no law." A spirituality is the terrain on which "the children of God" exercise their freedom (Rom. 8:21).

This freedom is one that must be put at the service of others (Gal. 5:13). This implies an apprenticeship that can be carried on only in the course of a journey, and this journey in turn is the total movement of a people that, like the prodigal son, confesses its waywardness, rises up, and goes to its Father (Luke 15:18). In all truth, the search for God is the ultimate meaning of any and every spirituality.

Encounter with Christ, life in the Spirit, journey to the Father: such, it seems to me, are the *dimensions* of every walking in the Spirit according to the scriptures. We shall verify this by a study of the texts. Let me say first, however, that we approach the Bible from our experience as believers and members of the church. It is in the light of that experience that we ask our questions.

Moreover we must not forget that the word of God issues its challenges. The scriptures are not a passive store of answers to our questions. We indeed read the Bible, but we can also say that the Bible "reads us." In many instances, our very questions will be reformulated. In the gospels this happens frequently to those who approach Jesus. For example, when Jesus is asked: "Who is my neighbor?" he reverses the terms of the question and inquires in turn: "Which of these three . . . proved neighbor to the man?" (Luke 10:29, 36).

The word of the Lord is abidingly new; it is a challenge that can radically change our lives, a grace that shakes us from our inertia, an answer that cannot be shackled by our questions. It is with this realization that we shall try to approach the texts of the Bible. A continual study of them will help us to understand the profound meaning of the experience of Christians in present-day Latin America.

3

ENCOUNTER WITH THE LORD

A spirituality is a walking in freedom according to the Spirit of love and life. This walking has its point of departure in an encounter with the Lord. Such an encounter is a spiritual experience that produces and gives meaning to the freedom of which I have been speaking. The encounter itself springs from the Lord's initiative. The scriptures state this repeatedly: "This is why I told you that no one can come to me unless it is granted him by the Father" (John 6:65). "You did not choose me, but I chose you" (John 15:16).

A spiritual experience, then, stands at the beginning of a spiritual journey.[1] That experience becomes the subject of later reflection and is proposed to the entire ecclesial community as a way of being disciples of Christ. The spirituality in question is therefore not, as is sometimes said, an application of a particular theology. Let me begin by clarifying this point.

Spirituality and Theology

The adoption of a spiritual perspective is followed by a reflection on faith (therefore, a theology) as lived in that perspective. This sequence is clear from the historical course followed in all the great spiritualities.[2]

I Believe in Order to Understand

Spiritual experience is the terrain in which theological reflection strikes root. Intellectual comprehension makes it possible to

35

carry the experience of faith to a deeper level, but the experience always comes first and is the source. St. Anselm (1033–1109) reminds us of this in a well-known passage:

> Lord, I do not attempt to comprehend Your sublimity, because my intellect is not at all equal to such a task. But I yearn to understand some measure of Your truth, which my heart believes and loves. For I do not seek to understand in order to believe but I believe in order to understand. For I believe even this: that I shall not understand unless I believe.[3]

I believe in order to understand. The level of the experience of faith supports a particular level of the understanding of faith. For theology is in fact a reflection that, even in its rational aspect, moves entirely within the confines of faith and direct testimony. "This is the disciple who is bearing witness to these things, and who has written these things; and we know that his testimony is true" (John 21:24).

In the gospels themselves, then, the experience of faith is presented as the starting point of all testimony and reflection:

> Inasmuch as many have undertaken to compile a narrative of the things which have been accomplished among us, just as they were delivered to us by those who were eyewitnesses and ministers of the word, it seemed good to me also, having followed all things closely for some times past, to write an orderly account for you, most excellent Theophilus, that you may know the truth concerning the things of which you have been informed [Luke 1:1–4].

As a matter of fact, in the early centuries every theology took the form of what we today call a "spiritual theology"—that is, it was a reflection carried on in function of the following of the Lord, the "imitation of Christ" *(imitatio Christi)*.[4] This integrated approach inspired the work of Thomas Aquinas who established a solid foundation for theology as a rationally organized body of knowledge.[5] But toward the fourteenth century a divorce began to take place between theology and spirituality that was to be harmful to both.

The solidity and energy of theological thought depend precisely on the spiritual experience that supports it. This experience takes the form, first and foremost, of a profound encounter with God and God's will.[6] Any discourse on faith starts from, and takes its bearings from, the Christian life of the community.[7] Any reflection that does not help in living according to the Spirit is not a Christian theology. When all is said and done, then, all authentic theology is spiritual theology. This fact does not weaken the rigorously scientific character of the theology; it does, however, properly situate it.

Spiritual Experience

At the root of every spirituality there is a particular experience that is had by concrete persons living at a particular time. The experience is both proper to them and yet communicable to others. I cited earlier the passage in St. Bernard of Clairvaux in which he says that in these matters all people should drink from their own well. The great spiritualities in the life of the church continue to exist because they keep sending their followers back to the sources.

The image of a well is used here because a spirituality is indeed like living water that springs up in the very depths of the experience of faith. John writes: "He who believes in me, as the scripture has said, 'Out of his heart shall flow rivers of living water' " (7:38). The life signified in the image of water comes to us through encounter with the Lord: "Whoever drinks of the water that I shall give him will never thirst; the water that I shall give him will become in him a spring of water welling up to eternal life" (John 4:14). In these texts "living water" refers to the gift of the Spirit that Jesus makes to his disciples.[8] Drinking from one's own well, then, is a "spirit-ual" experience in the fullest sense of the word. To have this experience is to live in the age of the Spirit and according to the Spirit.

As I shall have occasion to show in detail, what is going on today in Latin America makes it the place of an experience that is giving birth to a distinctive way of being Christian—that is, to a spirituality. This experience in turn is leaving its mark on the theological reflection that is springing out of all that is best in the Latin American church.

Such a statement does not in the least imply a forgetfulness of the task proper to a discourse on faith. All it does is make us aware that a theology that is not located in the context of an experience of faith is in danger of turning into a kind of religious metaphysics or a wheel that turns in the air without making the cart advance. Theological reflection takes on its full meaning only within the church and in the service of the life of the church and its action in the world.

This is what many Christians are now learning in Latin America. To be followers of Jesus requires that they walk with and be committed to the poor; when they do, they experience an encounter with the Lord who is simultaneously revealed and hidden in the faces of the poor (see Matt. 25:31–46, and the fine commentary in PD, nos. 31–39). This is a profound and demanding spiritual experience that serves as the point of departure for following Jesus and for reflection on his words and deeds.

See, Touch, Follow

The gospels present to us the experience that the disciples had of Jesus, and they do so with all the intimacy implied in the verbs "see," "hear," and "touch." To encounter the Lord is first of all to be encountered by the Lord. "You did not choose me, but I chose you and appointed you that you should go and bear fruit" (John 15:16). In this encounter we discover where the Lord lives and what the mission is that has been entrusted to us.

The here and now always puts its mark on this experience. And the experience calls for a testimony to it and a communication of it. " 'Do not hold me,' " Jesus says to Mary, " 'for I have not yet ascended to the Father; but go to my brethren and say to them, I am ascending to my Father and your Father, to my God and your God.' Mary Magdalene went and said to the disciples, 'I have seen the Lord'; and she told them that he had said things to her" (John 20:17–18). Here is the testimony to an unconditional life that gives full meaning to a shared filiation, which in its turn is the basis for human fellowship.

Where Are You Staying?

The gospels contain various stories about encounters with Jesus. Among these there is one in John that is especially penetrating and rich in meaning:

The next day again John was standing with two of his disciples; and he looked at Jesus as he walked, and said, "Behold the Lamb of God!"

The two disciples heard him say this, and they followed Jesus. Jesus turned, and saw them following, and said to them, "What do you seek?" And they said to him, "Rabbi" (which means Teacher), "where are you staying?" He said to them, "Come and see."

They came and saw where he was staying; and they stayed with him that day, for it was about the tenth hour.

One of the two who heard John speak, and followed him, was Andrew, Simon Peter's brother. He first found his brother Simon, and said to him, "We have found the Messiah" (which means Christ). He brought him to Jesus. Jesus looked at him, and said, "So you are Simon the son of John? You shall be called Cephas" (which means Peter) [John 1:35–42].

This simple sketch of an encounter (possibly that of John himself)[9] with the Lord becomes a paradigm for the many others that would take place in the lives of Christians of every age. It is important, therefore, to analyze it in some detail.

JOHN AND HIS DISCIPLES. According to the fourth Gospel, when John saw Jesus coming toward him he had said: "After me comes a man who ranks before me, for he was before me" (1:30). The forerunner steps aside and invites his disciples to follow the one whose way he had been preparing. The first disciples of Jesus come from the school of the Baptist. For a second time, John acknowledges Jesus, who has already begun to go his own way, as "the Lamb of God" (the first time was in v. 29). The echoes of the exodus that are so strong in the Gospel of John, especially in its early chapters, justify us in interpreting this original expression in the light of the Passover lamb "whose blood freed the people from death."[10] The Lamb of God is the sacrificial victim of the new covenant; his blood will be shed as that of the lambs of the old covenant had been. He is the Lamb that makes expiation, but also a victorious Lamb: the Apocalypse will show us "the four living creatures and the twenty-four elders" prostrating themselves before the Lamb, "and they sang a new song, saying, 'Worthy art thou to take the scroll and to open its seals, for thou wast slain and by thy blood didst ransom men for God from every tribe and tongue and people and nation' " (Rev. 5:8-9).

The two disciples follow Jesus. Before they do so they have been advised of the difficulties and conflicts they will face in taking the path of the Lamb of God. It is not an easy road, but one that leads through persecution and a martyr's death. The master does not hide this from them: "If they persecuted me, they will persecute you" (John 15:20). But the journey is also accompanied by the promise of final victory and the sovereign rule of the Lamb.

All this is included in the idea of following. The verb "to follow" is used in the gospels for the progression of disciples as they walk in the footsteps of the master. It signifies both the obedient acceptance of the Lord's call and the creativity required by the new way they are to travel.[11] Jesus says to Philip: "Follow me" (John 1:43; see also 8:12; 10:4; 12:26; 13:26; 21:9). The disciples here follow Jesus in silence, but it is a silence heavy with meaning, for their following is already an adherence of faith and an acceptance of the consequences the following entails. They have taken the first step in their "staying with" Jesus (John 1: 39).

TWO QUESTIONS AND AN ANSWER. Jesus breaks the silence of his followers and asks: "What do you seek?" (John 1:38). This formal question, direct and unavoidable, is meant to sound out the quality of the initial adhesion that the disciples of John have just given to the following of Jesus. Jesus puts them in the critical position of defining themselves from the outset. It is not enough simply to follow him, for there are forms of adhesion that are not reliable (John 2:23-25) and others that break down at the first demands of discipleship (Luke 9:61; 18:18-23). Jesus' question (the Greek text has the present tense: "he asks") is directed to all who claim to follow him, whatever the period of history to which they belong.

The term "Rabbi" occurs eight times in the Gospel of John; it is used seven times of Jesus and once (3:26) of John the Baptist. The word was currently applied to anyone regarded as a teacher, as a man learned in some area; it was applied chiefly, however, to anyone who taught by the witness he gave, by his manner of life. The question that the disciples ask in response to the question of Jesus takes that fact into account: "Where are you staying?"

(John 1:39). The disciples are here "inviting themselves" to intimacy with Jesus. Their question expresses their desire to be taught through sharing the life of Jesus. Their intention in following him is now clear.

One question has been answered by another. The dialogue has been short but complete. Jesus ends it with an explicit call to follow him; he invites the disciples to enter his own sphere, to come and see where he is staying, and to accept the consequences of such a coming and seeing. The text, however, makes no reference to any dwelling of Jesus, and there is nothing to keep us from thinking that this Galilean, this itinerant preacher, has no permanent abode. This is, in fact, what he himself says in the Gospel of Matthew: "Foxes have holes, and birds of the air have nests; but the Son of man has nowhere to lay his head" (8:20). His mission causes him to extend the boundaries of his dwelling and family; it is in that light that he sets down the condition for belonging to the community he is assembling: "Whoever does the will of my Father in heaven is my brother, and sister, and mother" (Matt. 12:50).

John himself, nonetheless, gives us a clue as to the dwelling of Jesus. He tells us in the Prologue of his Gospel: "And the Word became flesh and dwelt among us" (1:14). This is the place where Jesus dwells: the tent he has pitched in the midst of us, at the center of history. Jesus lives in his task of proclaiming the gospel, for that is where his Father's business is located (Luke 2:49).

This, then, is what the disciples saw and, because they decided to enlist for this work, they stayed with him from that day forward.[12] This passage in its bare simplicity tells us of the birth of a Christian community. Jesus and the two disciples, with others soon following, share a life. For all of them the following of Jesus entails a commitment to a mission that requires them, like their master, to pitch camp in the midst of human history and there give witness to the Father's love.

John did not forget the hour when he met Jesus: "It was about the tenth hour."[13] Like every event that leaves its mark on a human life, this encounter remained a detailed memory and made an indelible impression. The exact moment in time does not as such seem to have any significance for us today; after all, it would make no difference to us whether this encounter took place at ten in the morning or two in the afternoon. But the exact time certainly did have meaning for the person who experienced the event. The text bears witness to this; as a result the passage has a decidedly personal tone. In its very insignificance this mention of the tenth hour conveys a profound message, for we all have these "tenth hours" in our lives, intense moments of encounter with the Lord in which our spiritual lives are nourished. They are the well from which we drink every so often.

ENCOUNTER WITH THE MESSIAH. Encounter with the Lord is not restricted to the disciples, for the very nature of the event leads to communication, to witness. The former disciples of John the Baptist are fully conscious of the kind of encounter that has just taken place.

This is why they jointly recognize Jesus, whom they have called Rabbi, as the Messiah. That is, they recognize in him the only-begotten Son of God who has come in order to proclaim the good news of his reign. The community now beginning to take shape will be a messianic community whose task is to offer a specific witness in the midst of human history.

The following of Jesus is not, purely or primarily, an individual matter but a collective adventure. The journey of the people of God is set in motion by a direct encounter with the Lord but an encounter in community: "*We* have found the Messiah."

Bearing Witness to Life

The text I have been analyzing calls to mind two other New Testament passages that enable us to penetrate more deeply into the meaning of encounter with the Lord and the resultant following of him.

THE GOSPEL TO THE POOR. Matthew and Luke likewise tell us about an encounter of two disciples of John with Jesus. The emphases are not the same as in John's account; the tone is less personal, and the problems entailed in following are only implicit. The passages in Matthew and Luke do, however, add important details about the work of Jesus. When discussing the passage in John I said that in it we were not told where the Lord lives; I did, however, suggest that his mission gives a clue in this regard. The texts we shall now be considering are important precisely in this area. Let us start with the version of Matthew:

> Now when John heard in prison about the deeds of the Christ, he sent word by his disciples [var.: by two of his disciples] and said to him, "Are you he who is to come, or shall we look for another?"
>
> And Jesus answered them, "Go and tell John what you hear and see: the blind receive their sight and the lame walk, lepers are cleansed and the deaf hear, and the dead are raised up, and the poor have the good news preached to them. And blessed is he who takes no offense at me" [11:2-6].

As in the passage from the fourth Gospel, here again John sends two disciples to meet Jesus. Their purpose in this instance is to inquire whether Jesus is the Messiah or whether they must still wait for someone else. The reports the Baptist has heard have perplexed him to some extent, but they have also stirred up hope—and how could they fail to do so?

Again as in John, Jesus' answer takes the form of concrete witness. This time he bids the disciples, not to come after him and see, but to return to John the Baptist and tell him what they have seen and heard.[14] Jesus' works are to provide the answer to the question of his identity. They are works that match those foretold by Isaiah (61:1-2) in a passage that plays an important role in the gospels in defining the mission of the Messiah. Luke 4:16-20 makes use of the same passage in order to elicit from Jesus what has been called his "first messianic declaration."[15]

Works done to benefit the poor and needy identify Jesus as the Messiah, the same Messiah whom (in the passage from John) the disciples claim to have met. Perhaps these disciples had witnessed such works when they accepted the invitation to live with the Rabbi. The Son of Man who has no place to lay his head lives in these actions that manifest the breakthrough of the reign of God into the present age. That reign is meant first and foremost for the poor and then, through them, for every human being.

The cures of which the parallel passages in Matthew and Luke speak are an anticipation and pledge of that reign. The alleviation of the suffering of *some* of the poor in the time of Jesus is a sure promise that the good news of the reign of God is being proclaimed to *all* the poor of history. It is a proclamation through liberating words and liberating actions. The gospel is proclaimed to the poor by means of concrete deeds. When Jesus made human beings see and walk and hear and, in short, gave them life, he was giving an example for that time and a mandate to the Christian community throughout history. This is what is meant by "remembering the poor," and it is something we should be "eager to do" (Gal. 2:10). There is no authentic evangelization that is not accompanied by action in behalf of the poor.

The cures reported give full meaning to the good news for the poor that is promised in Isaiah and that becomes a reality through the messianic activity of Jesus.[16] But this method of revealing his messiahship will not be readily understood, and this is why the passage ends in a beatitude: "Blessed is he who takes no offense at me."

It is in this messianic work that Jesus has his dwelling. It is in this work that worship "in Spirit and truth" is to be offered (John 4:23). Happy they who do not take offense but instead accept the invitation to follow Jesus and live with him.

THE LIFE WAS MADE MANIFEST. The second passage of which the meeting of the Baptist's disciples with Jesus reminds us comes from the Johannine writings and deals with the necessity of sharing with others the experience of the Lord:

> That which was from the beginning,
> which we have heard,
> which we have seen with our eyes,
> which we have looked upon and touched with our
>   hands,
> concerning the word of life—
> the life was made manifest,
> and we saw it, and testify to it,
> and proclaim to you the eternal life
> which was with the Father
> and was made manifest to us—
> that which we have seen and heard
> we proclaim also to you,
> so that you may have fellowship with us;
> and our fellowship
> is with the Father and with his Son Jesus Christ.
> And we are writing this
> that our joy may be complete [1 John 1:1–4].

What we proclaim (says the writer) is what we have heard and seen and looked upon and touched with our hands. These are direct, unmediated experiences that are communicated in order that others too may have the joy of encountering the Lord. The gospels are full of such testimonies (Luke 2:16-17, 38; John 4:28; 20:17-18). What is manifested in this way is life. That is the content of the reign of the Father, the living God who raises Jesus to life and thus overcomes death once and for all.

A follower of Jesus is a witness to life. This statement takes on a special meaning in Latin America where the forces of death have created a social system that marginalizes the very poor who have a privileged place in the kingdom of life. The passage from 1 John gives us a better understanding of what we call nowadays the spiritual life: life according to the Spirit, life lived in love. Recall that in this same Letter John speaks to us the final word about God: "God is love" (1 John 4:8). The follower of Jesus must therefore not live in fear: fear, according to John, is the opposite of the love that sets us free (1 John 4:18).

Anyone who has met the Lord "has the Son" and "has life" (1 John 5:12). Witness must be borne to this.

Acknowledging the Messiah

To give witness to life implies passage through death. This experience, which marks the present Latin American situation, is an ineluctable consequence of the encounter with and acknowledgment of Jesus as the Messiah, of whom the texts of John and Matthew speak. This is not something easy for a follower to accept. A text from Mark will help us to understand this point:

> And Jesus went on with his disciples, to the villages of Caesarea Philippi; and on the way he asked his disciples, "Who do men say that I am?" And they told him, "John the Baptist; and others say, Elijah; and others one of the prophets." And he asked them, "But who do you say that I am?" Peter answered him, "You are the Christ." And he charged them to tell no one about him.
>
> And he began to teach them that the Son of Man must suffer many things, and be rejected by the elders and the chief priests

and the scribes, and be killed, and after three days rise again. And he said this plainly. And Peter took him, and began to rebuke him. But turning and seeing his disciples, he rebuked Peter, and said, "Get behind me, Satan! For you are not on the side of God, but of men."

And he called to him the multitude with his disciples, and said to them, "If any man would come after me, let him deny himself and take up his cross and follow me" [Mark 8:27–35].

This passage occupies a central place in the evangelist's narrative. It is the culminating moment of what is called the "messianic secret" in Mark: when someone recognizes that Jesus is the Messiah, he orders that person not to tell it further.[17]

The affirmation that Jesus of Nazareth is the Messiah, the Christ, is the nucleus of christological faith. The first sentence in Mark's Gospel reads: "The beginning of the gospel of Jesus Christ, the Son of God" (1:1); John's Gospel ends: "These are written that you may believe that Jesus is the Christ, the Son of God, and that believing you may have life in his name" (20:31). According to Luke this affirmation is a resumé of Peter's preaching to the Jews among the newer members of the comunity of believers: "Let all the house of Israel therefore know assuredly that God has made him both Lord and Christ, this Jesus whom you crucified" (Acts 2:36).

To profess "this Jesus," to acknowledge "Jesus the Christ," is to express a conviction. It is not simply putting a name and a title together; it is an authentic confession of faith. It is the assertion of an identity: the Jesus of history, the son of Mary, the carpenter of Nazareth, the preacher of Galilee, the crucified, *is* the Only Begotten of God, the Christ, the Son of God.

An Interrogation

In Mark's text, the question "Who do you say that I am?" does not come from the crowd or from Jesus' disciples (as in John 1:39 and Matthew 11:3); it comes from Jesus himself. It is directed to those who have accompanied him for some time and have been witnesses of his words and deeds. The question is not, therefore, directed to persons who do not know him or who have had little contact with him. It is directed to those who have reason to know something about him because they have followed him. They are his disciples.

It is a question that looks for a profession of faith, though, in other contexts, it sometimes elicits an answer that includes an element of doubt or perplexity. The language is direct and leaves no room for evasion. And it is not directed to one person, but to the disciples conjointly ("you" in the plural). Profession of faith will be communal, as will also the expression of doubt or perplexity.

The interrogation is twofold, looking for two answers. The first question asks what others say about Jesus. His mission has been public; the crowds can be expected to have—and certainly do have—some ideas about him. What is asked, then, is how the disciples interpret what they have heard; what impact it has had on them. This is a question, then, about the faith of the disciples themselves: what others have learned in the faith is an aspect of our own faith. Knowledge of Jesus, then and now, does not rely only on what believers have seen for themselves, but also on what they perceive in those who say they are his followers. And Mark, in chapter 6, has already narrated the sending of the disciples on an evangelical mission (6:6–13). The question, then, is: What testimony have you given of me?

This first question is not simply a stepping stone to the second question. It is a question in its own right, a question about the lived faith of the members of his immediate circle of companions. When we refer to what others think, we always show what *we* think: we accept an opinion, or take distance from it, or refute it.

This is a good opportunity for us to recall that the answer to the question about Jesus is not something that pertains to us in a private capacity. Nor does it pertain only to the church. Christ stands beyond its frontiers and questions all humankind, as Vatican II clearly reminded us. "Who do they say that I am?" is a question that, precisely because it escapes private or ecclesiastical confines, retains its validity for the community of yesterday and today. It is important for ecclesial faith to know what others think about Jesus, and how our testimony as disciples is received. To know how to listen will help us to make a better and more efficacious proclamation of our faith in the Lord vis-à-vis the world.[18]

The text continues: "They told him, 'John the Baptist . . . Eli-

jah . . . one of the prophets.' ''[19] It is significant that the
crowds—at least from what the disciples here report—did not
think that Jesus was the Messiah.[20] In the text we are pondering, it
does not seem that political messianism played a major role
among the populace.

Matthew, in a parallel text, adds the name of Jeremiah to that
of Elijah. All three mentioned are important in the religious history of the Jewish people. We are given an interpretation of the
new (Jesus) on the basis of what is already known (persons of the
past). This is a spontaneous procedure, often resorted to. And, in
this case, it includes an evaluation, given the significance of the
persons mentioned, although it does not evince a perception of
the newness brought by Jesus. But it points to a fertile terrain:
John the Baptist, Elijah, and Jeremiah were prophets. If Jesus is
not sketched in all his singularity, what is implied is something
freighted with consequences; Jesus is perceived as within the prophetic line, that which speaks "in the name of God." Jesus is
given a high place in having his preaching associated with the
great prophetic perspective of Israel. But this does not tell everything.

The second question has more of a bite to it and goes much
deeper: Who do *you* say that I am? You; not the others. As
before, what is asked refers to an objective reality, something
exterior to the disciples: Jesus asks them, Who am I? Diverse ap-
proximations can be given, but they are all concerned with a
unique reality that stands beyond human opinion: the reality,
the presence, of the Lord. The question pulls us out of our
subjective world and, "turning us inside out," locates the point
of reference of our faith, and of our life, beyond ourselves, in
the person of Jesus.

The answer will have to have the seal of objectivity. But the
question is directed to "you" (in the plural), and its answer will be
made by them and consequently will be shaped by their way of
viewing Jesus. Firstly and most basically, the answer depends on
what is asked; but it also depends on who is being asked. Knowing
Jesus has an impact on all the aspects of our existence, and they
will all be present in the response that we give.

The text continues with the clear confession of Peter in the
name of the other apostles: "You are the Christ." Not simply a

prophet, as the crowds thought, but the Only Begotten of God, the Christ, he in whom God's promises are realized.[21] Mark writes his gospel in the light of this acknowledgment, and synthesizes the faith of the disciples, yet insists once more: "He charged them to tell no one about him."[22]

Lived Response

What follows is decisive. Jesus reveals something new: "the Son of Man must suffer many things, and be rejected by the elders and the chief priests and the scribes, and be killed, and after three days rise again." This was something he had not revealed until that moment: that his mission would be rejected by those held in respect (the elders, chief priests, and scribes—that is, the Sanhedrin), and this rejection will lead to his death. Peter, who had just acknowledged Jesus to be the Messiah, refuses to accept the conflictual part of Jesus' mission. What distrubs Peter is not the failure of his mission—given that Jesus speaks also of his resurrection "after three days"—but the conflict and suffering that had to be endured.

Jesus' reply is radical: "Get behind me, Satan."[23] The expression *upage opiso mou*, "get behind me," could mean "take up again your post as a disciple and do not be an obstacle (Satan) in my way." The place for the disciple of Jesus is behind him, behind the Master. So interpreted, what seems a harsh reprimand is really a call to return to the path of discipleship. So taken—although there is little in the text itself to necessitate this interpretation—it implies confidence in Peter's capacity to realign himself with the followers of the Master. Peter's reluctance to accept the consequences that accrue to messiahship for Jesus and his followers is flatly rejected. Peter, even though he had made himself worthy of being compared to Satan, receives a call that includes a pardon. Jesus' reprimand comports the admixture of mitigation.

We are here touching on a central point in belief in Jesus. This text has often been interpreted to mean that Peter's resistance stems from a political conceptualization of the Messiah. Jesus, by contrast, here reveals that his mission is spiritual. The disciples were given a progressive enlightenment on this truth (Mark

10:35–45). It must also be seen in a broader and deeper perspective, that of the rejection of the nationalist and zealot conceptualization of the Messiah.[24] Mark writes from this perspective. But he and the other evangelists also make clear that the reasons for Jesus' confrontation with the powerful of his day are to be found in the proclamation of the good news of the Father's love of all humankind, especially the poor. This marks the character of Jesus' messiahship. What was rejected in him, and led to his death on the cross, was the same nucleus of his teaching: the kingdom of God.

Jesus' concrete form of proclaiming the gratuitous love of God and the kingdom had inevitable consequences for the religious, social, and economic order prevailing in his time. "They watched him" and planned his execution (Mark 3:1–6). At bottom, the conflict and suffering that Peter reacted to ("and all of us with him!") were provoked by that same mission. Hostility did not arise because the teaching of the Messiah was political (which it clearly was not, particularly in the strict sense of the term), but precisely because it was a religious teaching that affected all human existence.

What prompted Peter's rejection was his reluctance to accept the consequences of acknowledging that Jesus is the Christ. Verses 34 and 35 spell out the requirements of the following of Jesus. This is what Peter balked at. It is not enough to recognize that Jesus is the Christ; it is necessary to accept all that that implies. To believe in Christ is also to assume his practice. A profession of faith without practice is incomplete, as stated in Matthew, "Not everyone who says to me 'Lord, Lord,' shall enter the kingdom of heaven, but he who does the will of my Father who is in heaven" (7:21) Orthodoxy, correct opinion, demands orthopraxis: comportment in accord with the opinion expressed.

The practice of the following of Jesus will show what lies behind the acknowledgment of the Messiah. It will show whether our thoughts are those of God or only our own (Mark 8:33) —the ideas we have of Jesus and of our discipleship. It is in our historical following—in our walking the path of Jesus—that the final judgment on our faith in Christ will be made. The following of Jesus is the solid ground on which can be built a reflection on Jesus as the Christ, a christology; otherwise it

will be built on sand. In theology, as in all intellectual elabora-
tion, critical thought is required. In our undertaking, the critique
that comes from practice—the following of Jesus—cannot be left
out.

To the question "Who do you say that I am?" we cannot give a
merely theoretical or theological answer. What answers it, in the
final analysis, is our life, our personal history, our manner of
living the gospel.

Peter's affirmation, "You are the Christ," is fundamental. But
what is demanded is that we make that affirmation the guiding
thought of our life—accepting all the consequences, as dire as
they may be.[25] Only so is our response valid, as honest and sincere
as it may be without it. Our response to the question, "Who do
you say that I am?" does not end with a profession of faith or a
theological systemization. It is a question addressed to our life
and that of the entire church. It permanently tests the Christian
faith, leading it to its ultimate consequences.

The final verses of the text spell out the consequences of the
following of Jesus. "Taking up the cross" can be a rich metaphor, and it is often taken in that sense.[26] But that is not its only
interpretation. It can also point to a shocking reality: condemnation to death on the cross. Jesus' contemporaries were well aware
of that reality; they knew of crucifixions ordered and imposed on
Jewish soil by the Roman overlords.[27] It would take place a little
later for Jesus himself. The experience of martyrdom lived
in Latin America heightens and sharpens this meaning of the
text.

The true disciple must, therefore, be prepared to confront a like
situation. Such preparation is not an easy matter. Peter's
reaction—measured by our profession of the faith—is an abiding
possibility. It expresses itself in subtle and cunning ways. The testimony of numerous Latin Americans makes this possibility
manifest, but it also makes us realize that there are some who have
determined to put themselves behind Jesus and follow him, paying the price of rejection, of calumny, or even of the surrender of
their own lives. Those who lose their life for the Lord and the
gospel will save it. The following of Jesus is oriented to the horizon of resurrection, definitive life.

Encounter, Experience, Reflection, Prolongation

Every great spirituality begins with the attainment of a certain level of experience. Then follows reflection on this experience, thus making it possible to propose it to the Christian community as a way of following Christ.

I Will Come in to Him and Eat with Him (Rev. 3:20)

The initiative in encounter belongs to the Lord. But if we open the door of our being to him, we shall share his life, his supper. In every spiritual history there is an initial moment that is a kind of "heroic age." At that moment, in a particular historical context, a fruitful spiritual experience takes place. To cite one example: Ignatius of Loyola was referring to such a moment when, in thinking back on his experiences at Pamplona and Manresa, he spoke of his "primitive church."[28]

Such an experience is not only a point of departure but a permanent wellspring of life. Thus the first Christian community possessed an archetypal quality and has left an indelible mark on the memory and imagination of the church as having been a privileged moment of grace, discovery, searching, and life—both with the Lord and with brothers and sisters (Acts 2:41–47). So too the "primitive church" of Ignatius is equivalent to the "tenth hour" of which I spoke earlier. It is the well from which we must drink. Such experiences are the source of a great spiritual freedom.[29]

Theology Comes Afterward

I made this point above. In a second moment, spiritual experience becomes a subject for reflection; it is "theologized," turned into theology. This makes it easier to communicate experience as well as to exercise discernment regarding it. The history of the Christian community offers us many examples of this sequence.

Albert the Great (1206–1280) and Thomas Aquinas (1224–1274) come after Dominic Guzmán (1173–1221), reflect on his experience, and give it the support of solid theological research. Something similar is true in the relationship between Bonaventure (1217–1274) and Francis of Assisi (1181–1226). The spirituality of the mendicant orders, focusing on the poverty of the church, is buttressed by theologies that help it establish a fuller contact with the biblical sources and with the culture of the age. The same thing happened to Ignatius of Loyola (1491–1556), who found among his first disciples some distinguished theologians, Diego Laínez (1512–1565) and Jerónimo Nadal (1507–1570), for example, who went back over his spiritual intuitions and reflected systematically on them (as a matter of fact, Ignatius himself had already done this to some extent).

Examples might be multiplied, but these will suffice. All of them manifest basically the sequence I have pointed out. To reflect theologically on a spiritual experience means to work through it by relating it to the word of the Lord, to the thinking of one's own age, and to other ways of understanding the following of Jesus.

For the Building Up of the Church (1 Cor. 14:12)

A spiritual experience and the ensuing reflection on it are not the end of the line; that would be a denial of their very meaning. On the contrary, they are offered to the ecclesial community as a way of being Christian.

As *a,* not *the,* way of being Christian. A spirituality is only one expression of that diversity of charisms in the church of which Paul speaks so often (e.g., 1 Cor. 12). I might compare what happens to spiritualities in the history of the church to what happens to biological species in the history of a phylum: the strongest survive. Spiritualities come down through the centuries and continually serve as appropriate ways of following Jesus.

This means that such spiritualities as the Franciscan, the Dominican, the Ignatian, or the Carmelite still have much to say to us. The depth of the spiritual experience from which they sprang, as well as the amplitude of the theological reflection that they inspired, have kept them alive.

4

WALKING ACCORDING TO THE SPIRIT

The initial encounter with the Lord is the starting point of a *following,* or discipleship. The journeying that ensues is what St. Paul calls "walking according to the Spirit" (Rom. 8:4). It is also what we today speak of as a *spirituality.*

The term "spirituality" is a relatively recent one in the history of the church. It came into use around the beginning of the seventeenth century in French religious circles at a time that saw a wealth of contributions and works on the subject. Everything that had to do with Christian perfection fell under the heading of *spiritual life*, whereas reflection of the subject yielded a *spiritual theology.*[1]

These expressions, which are meant to explicate the meaning of the ancient and classical "following of Jesus," give pride of place to a traditional and fruitful term: spiritual. Everyone is familiar with the biblical basis for the word as well as with the frequent use made of it in any consideration of Christian life. It is indeed a central and rich concept, but also, it must be acknowledged, one open to equivocations that unfortunately have darkened many periods of the history of spirituality.

I made reference to these confusions in chapter 1. It is important, therefore, to go back to the biblical sources as well as to the authors of the great spiritualities, and to refine our understanding of certain ideas. One of the chief causes of equivocation is, for example, the use of the distinction, so predominant in Western culture, between body and soul as a tool for interpreting expressions used in scripture.

But the possibilities of getting ourselves launched on doubtful paths should not allow us to lose sight of the deep meaning of what Paul calls "walking according to the Spirit." By this he means a life proper to the follower of Jesus and opposed to ways of life inspired by other perspectives. The disciple of the Lord lives in and according to the Spirit who is freedom and love because the Spirit is *life*, and not according to the "flesh," which is law and sin because it is *death*. Jesus himself promises us the gift of the Spirit, which is to accompany us on the road that leads us to "all the truth" (John 16:13). The presence of the Spirit sets the "messianic people" (*Lumen gentium*, no. 9) in motion for its quest of God.

Although life according to the Spirit is a theme throughout the entire New Testament (the same was already true to some extent in the Old Testament), I shall draw my texts chiefly from Paul. For it is undoubtedly he who gives the fullest and most profound treatment of it, though also the one on which scholars are least in agreement. *Flesh*, *spirit*, and *body* are terms in his writings that have left a definitive mark on Christian life and thought. The words carry multiple and complex meanings that also overlap and need to be disentangled. Terminological analysis alone is not enough; unless we take into account the major axes of Pauline theology we shall not fully grasp the meaning of these three ideas. An approach by way of Pauline theology will also help us to keep the interpretation flexible and avoid reifying realities that are fluid and at times elusive.

In the following pages I shall take as a guiding thread two important and well-known passages: Romans 8 and its parallel, Galatians 5. In these passages we have a brilliant synthesis of the following of Jesus as a life according to the Spirit. Other texts from the letters of Paul will be cited in complementary reference to these two central passages.[2]

The Flesh of Death

The word "flesh," and its derivatives, show a variety of meanings in the Bible and especially in Paul.[3] But at the same time the meanings form a graduated and profoundly unified series. It is not easy to locate accurately the point of transition from one meaning to another, but the important thing is not to lose sight of the all-inclusive series within which each is located and which gives the semantic field of the term its proper and distinctive character.

The Hebrew word *basar* is translated into Greek both by *sarx* (flesh) and *soma* (body).[4] The idea of "body" constitutes one of the main axes of Pauline theology[5] and I shall study it a little further on; first, however, let us look at the scope of the idea of "flesh."

All Flesh

The word "flesh" signifies first of all the substance of which human beings are made: "Not all flesh is alike, but there is one kind for men, another for animals" (1 Cor. 15:39). Moreover it describes not a *part* of the human person, but the *whole* of the person as seen in terms of its physical existence. Thus Paul speaks of his "flesh" as synonymous with his person: "A thorn was given me in the flesh . . . to keep me from being too elated" (2 Cor. 12:7; cf. 2 Cor. 7:5; Gal. 4:14; Col. 1:24; Col. 2:1, 5). He will speak in the same way of other persons (see 1 Cor. 7:28; Eph. 5:28). To say, then, that no flesh is present is to say that no one is there (Rom. 3:20; Gal. 2:16; 1 Cor. 1:29).[6] Paul regards Onesimus as a brother "both in the flesh and in the Lord" (Philem. 16)— that is, as a human being and as a Christian. The flesh is thus not a component joined to the spirit or soul in order to make up a human person.[7] The entire human being is flesh when looked at from a particular point of view.

It is important to note that these uses of the word "flesh" carry no moral qualification or pejorative overtone. All that is meant is the human being insofar as it is a material, corporeal, carnal creature. In the Semitic outlook the flesh is a component in human solidarity; it is an earthly tie. To be of the same flesh means to belong to the same ethnic group, the same people, and, in the final analysis, the same human family. To live "in the flesh" ("If it is to be life in the flesh, that means fruitful labor for me": Phil. 1:22) is, therefore, to share the human condition. In this perspective, being linked to another "according to the flesh" means sharing the same lineage. The Messiah is descended from the patriarchs "according to the flesh" (Rom. 9:5; cf. 1:3).

In addition, then, to signifying the person taken as a whole, "flesh" expresses—and this is important—a bond of human solidarity at the physical level. It implies a collective dimension that is typical of biblical thinking and has important consequences for a spiritual perspective.[8]

The Flesh Is Weak

But we have not said everything about the meaning of the term. "Flesh" also signifies aspects of weakness and mortality that in turn entail a certain distance and difference with respect to God and God's power. To say that human beings are flesh is to say that they are created by God; now we must add that as flesh they are also weak and mortal.

Because human beings are of flesh, they are weak: "I am speaking in human terms because of your natural limitations [lit.: the weakness of your flesh]" (Rom. 6:19). They are also superficial and likely to equivocate: "Was I vacillating when I wanted to do this? Do I make my plans like a worldly man [lit.: according to the flesh], ready to say Yes and No at once?" (2 Cor. 1:17). They are likely to prove weak: "You know it was because of a bodily ailment [lit.: a weakness of the flesh] that I preached my gospel to you at first" (Gal. 4:13). And, finally, they are subject to physical death (2 Cor. 4:11).

At this level, the phrase "according to the flesh" is used of acting in accordance with purely human criteria and thus in ways subject to the ambiguities mentioned. Paul says, for example, that he counts on acting with determination "against some who suspect us of acting in worldly fashion [lit.: according to the flesh]" (2 Cor. 10:2; cf. 2:17). A wisdom according to the flesh is a purely human wisdom but not therefore lacking in dignity: "Not many of you were wise according to worldly standards [lit.: according to the flesh]" (1 Cor. 1:26; cf. 2 Cor. 1:12).

The weakness inherent in the flesh is what makes the human person liable to be snared by sin. But to go fully into this aspect would be to move on to another point in the series of meanings that the word "flesh" has. Let me observe simply that here again the weakness in question affects not a part of the human being but the being as a whole and that in this too a kind of human communion exists. There is a solidarity in inherent weakness.

A Death-Dealing Power

Up to this point the concepts I have been examining have firm roots in the Old Testament. But Paul takes a further step that, though in profound continuity with what has gone before, represents a contribution of his own that will have its impact on the whole set of meanings that I have been reviewing.[9] Paul connects the flesh with sin, the law, and, in short, death.

In the final analysis the human person is to be defined by relationship to God. This relationship is marked, however, by a profound ambiguity that is expressed, for Paul, in the conflict of flesh and spirit: "The desires of the flesh are against the Spirit, and the desires of the Spirit are against the flesh; for these are opposed to each other" (Gal. 5:17). Flesh and spirit are correlative ideas. To place our trust in God and act accordingly is, in Paul's view, to be "spiritual." To give our lives to what is not God and, in the final analysis, to make ourselves the supreme norm of our conduct is to act "carnally"—that is, to behave sinfully: "Sending his own Son in the likeness of sinful flesh and for sin, he [God] condemned sin in the flesh" (Rom. 8:3). Flesh here is "the flesh of sin" or "sinful flesh."

We have here another aspect or nuance in the complete idea of "flesh." This aspect is undoubtedly linked to the others but it is also distinct from them within what I have been calling the gamut or range of meanings. Flesh comes on the scene here as a force for evil that lays hold of human beings and subjects them to its own desires: "Those who act according to the flesh set their minds on the things of the flesh, but those who live according to the Spirit set their minds on the things of the Spirit" (Rom. 8:5; in Gal. 5:13 Paul speaks of "not using your freedom as an opportunity for the flesh"). This possession of human persons by the power of death locates them in a kind of domain of sin that is set over against God: "Those who are in the flesh cannot please God" (Rom. 8:8). Being "in the flesh" (*en sarki*) is opposed to what Paul calls being "in Christ" (Rom. 8:1) or "in the Spirit" ("But you are not in the flesh, you are in the Spirit" [Rom. 8:9]) and therefore in a different domain or sphere.

The domain of the flesh is a world that rejects God and God's will for our lives: "The mind that is set on the flesh is hostile to God; it does not submit to God's law" (Rom. 8:7). To walk according to the flesh (*kata sarka*) is to reject the presence of the Lord. It is to turn the flesh into the norm of behavior; this acceptance of a norm is necessarily translated into *works* or concrete forms of behavior. "Now the works of the flesh are plain: immorality, impurity, licentiousness, idolatry, sorcery, enmity, strife, jealousy, anger, selfishness, dissension, party spirit, envy, drunkenness, carousing, and the like" (Gal. 5:19–21).

This list contains not only actions that we today would think of as "carnal" but others we would regard as "spiritual": enmity, jealousy, envy, and so on. The reason is that, as in the earlier two meanings of flesh, so in this one the word refers not to a *part* of the human being but to its *entirety*. The "works of the flesh" are the actions of the person taken as a unit but subject to sin and therefore in a state of enmity toward other human beings and toward God (Rom. 8:7).[10] In all three meanings of "flesh" we thus find the same perspective: the unity and wholeness of the human person as seen by Paul. This is a fundamental datum in reading Paul.

What, in the final analysis, does "walking according to the flesh" mean at this level? Paul gives a categorical and enlightening answer: *the flesh leads to death.* "To set the mind on the flesh is death" (Rom. 8:6); such is the real dynamism of the flesh. The list of "works of the flesh" is proof of this, for they are all negations of love and ultimately of life. Consequently, those who do them "shall not inherit the kingdom of God" (Gal. 5:21)—that is, life. In other words, "to live according to the flesh" (Rom. 8:12) is not to live at all but to die; "for if you live according to the flesh you will die" (Rom. 8:13). Paul uses the expression "living according to the flesh" by way of contrast to "walking according to the Spirit," which means: advancing toward life.

Among the works of the flesh there is one, idolatry (Gal. 5:20), that clearly brings out this meaning because throughout the Bible idolatry is associated with death and with blood spilled unjustly.

This is true in particular of a form of idolatry that is specially singled out in the Gospel of Matthew and in Paul himself: trust in money. "You cannot serve God and mammon [money]," Jesus warns in the gospel of Matthew (6:24); Paul twice tells us that covetousness is idolatry (Col. 3:5; Eph. 5:5). To the idol wealth is sacrificed the blood of human victims that is shed through robbery, through contempt for the most elementary rights, and through every kind of oppression of the poor by the mighty. The prophet Ezekiel had long ago issued this denunciation: "Her princes in the midst of her are like wolves tearing the prey, shedding blood, destroying lives to get dishonest gain. . . . The people of the land have practiced extortion and committed robbery; they have oppressed the poor and needy, and have extorted from the sojourner without redress" (Ezek. 22:27, 29). On various occasions the scriptures portray oppressors as causing the death of the poor out of sheer voracity: "Have they no knowledge, all the evil-doers who eat up my people as they eat bread, and do not call upon the Lord?" (Ps. 14:4).[11]

To walk according to the flesh (Rom. 8:4) is to refuse "to serve Christ our Lord"; it is to attend rather to one's own interests—something for which Paul has a strong image: "to serve their own belly" (Rom. 16:18, literal). More than that, such persons make their own self-centeredness—their belly—into an idol, a false god. Such, in practice, is the lifestyle of the "enemies of the cross of Christ. Their end is destruction, their god is the belly, and they glory in their shame, with minds set on earthly things" (Phil. 3:18–19). We already know that to put one's trust in what is not God is to fall into idolatry (an ever present possibility in the life of a believer); it is a work of the flesh and as such leads to death.

The adjective "carnal, fleshly" is therefore a term that is used to express the human self-sufficiency that Pauls calls, for example, "fleshy wisdom" (2 Cor. 1:12, literal). This confinement within the self is a denial of others and of God; it is a rejection of love as what ultimately gives meaning to human existence. It therefore signifies death.

The flesh is thus seen as a power that acts upon human beings and that with their complicity—a combination of weakness and culpable acceptance—brings them into the kingdom of death.

This experience of complicity causes the Apostle to exclaim in a much quoted passage: "I do not understand my own actions. For I do not do what I want, but I do the very thing I hate" (Rom. 7:15).[12] He does, in other words, that which is utterly opposed to the very thing to which God destines him (the very thing to which he is "heir"): the kingdom of life. At this point we are faced with a clear opposition between flesh and Spirit.

I have devoted this section to specifying the meaning of the first of the two terms the "flesh" and "spirit"; in doing so I have limited myself to the abiding contrast Paul establishes between the two. Let me turn now to an examination of the meaning of "spirit" in Pauline theology.

The Spirit of Life

The word *spirit* (Latin: *spiritus*; Greek: *pneuma*; Hebrew: *ruah*) initially signifies natural phenomena: the wind and the breathing of human beings. The reference is therefore to something dynamic, but with the connotation of unobtrusiveness and even being difficult to grasp with the senses, and thus almost of invisibility and impalpableness. When we turn to Paul's use of the word we find ourselves faced once again with a range of overlapping meanings, such as we saw in discussing "flesh." I shall try to present this set of meanings without rigidifying words that in fact are used in subtle ways and with a wealth of nuances. Once again there is a basic assertion that gives a deeper unity to the entire set of meanings: "The Spirit is life" (Rom. 8:10, literal).

The Human Spirit

In many passages of Paul "spirit" designates not a part of the human person but the person as a whole. "For they [certain Christians] refreshed my spirit as well as yours" (1 Cor. 16:18)—that is, they refreshed me and you, the word "spirit" here replacing the personal pronouns. "The Lord be with your spirit" (2 Tim. 4:22)—that is, with you. "My mind [lit.: spirit] could not rest because I did not find my brother Titus there" (2 Cor. 2:13);

"my spirit" here is equivalent to "I" (cf. 1 Cor. 5:3; 7:34; 2 Cor. 7:1, 13; Col. 2:5).[13]

In this usage the human person is looked upon as a totality, but in the perspective of its dynamism, the "breath" that inspires its actions. "Spirit" therefore also signifies the attitude adopted by the person; it includes both the I and its intentions: "For God is my witness, whom I serve with my spirit in the gospel of his Son" (Rom. 1:9); "For God did not give us a spirit of timidity but a spirit of power and love and self-control" (2 Tim. 1:7). In the same order of ideas: "You did not receive the spirit of slavery to fall back into fear" (Rom. 8:15). This dynamism stands in contrast to the passivity and even weakness of the human person that are conveyed by the word "flesh."[14]

The Human Person under Grace

The dynamism and vitality expressed by "spirit" are accentuated when the human person is considered from the standpoint of God's action on it. Spirit and its derivates signify a life that is in accordance with God's will—that is, a life in accordance with the gift of divine filiation that finds expression in human fellowship.

In this context the spirit is the subject that receives the gifts of God: "The grace of the Lord Jesus Christ be with your spirit, brethren" (Gal. 6:18)—that is, with you (as we saw above), but with the connotation of you-as-receptive to divine grace (cf. Phil. 4:23). The first of these gifts of the Spirit is love (*agape*). "The fruit of the Spirit is love, joy, peace, patience, kindness, goodness, faithfulness, gentleness, self-control; against such there is no law" (Gal. 5:22–23). This fruit (*karpos*) of the Spirit is the opposite of the works (*erga*) of the flesh that we saw reviewed in the previous section.[15]

Love is the central gift and in a way contains all the others: "I appeal to you, brethren, by our Lord Jesus Christ and by the love of the Spirit, to strive together with me in your prayers to God on my behalf" (Rom. 15:30). Love alone will remain (1 Cor. 13) and for this reason is the first gift that should be sought: "Make love your aim, and earnestly desire the spiritual gifts, especially that you may prophesy" (1 Cor. 14:1).[16]

Love is a source of dynamic activity and life. The power of the Spirit leads to love of God and others and not to the working of miracles. This is why the purpose of the charisms is the building up of the community: "To each is given the manifestation of the Spirit for the common good" (1 Cor. 12:7). It is this ability to love that basically constitutes the power of spiritual persons who leave behind them the weakness of the flesh (Rom. 8:3). Brotherhood and sisterhood are based on divine sonship and daughterhood. Therefore "it is the Spirit himself [who] bear[s] witness with our spirit that we are children of God" (Rom. 8:16) and enables us to turn to God with the cry: "Abba! Father!" (Gal. 4:6; Rom. 8:15). The Spirit of [adoptive] filiation does not cancel out the human personality (the Spirit "bears witness *with* our spirit"), but gives it a new life. By reason of this life we are able to address God in the familiar word *Abba*, "papa," that Jesus used.[17] The term expresses an intimate union with God, with whom we form a single spirit: "He who is united to the Lord becomes one spirit with him" (1 Cor. 6:17).

Filiation and fellowship are the two dimensions of a life centered on the Spirit. But this life is a process, a journey; we have not yet fully attained the goal: We "groan inwardly as we wait for adoption as sons and daughters" (Rom. 8:23). At present we "have [only] the first fruits of the Spirit" (ibid.). Furthermore, it is possible to retrogress on the journey (1 Cor. 3:1). Flesh and spirit are not juxtaposed domains, but are principles of activity that give rise to processes that in all their manifestations intermesh in the life of the Christian.[18]

The ultimate meaning of this "walking according to the Spirit" (Rom. 8:4; Gal. 5:16, 25) is life, inasmuch as "the Spirit is life" (Rom. 8:10, literal). The goal is life, not death: "To set the mind on the flesh is death, but to set the mind on the Spirit is life and peace" (Rom. 8:6). That which, under the influence of the indwelling Spirit of God, undertakes this journey toward life is not a component *part* of the human being that alone would deserve the name "spirit"; it is the human person as a totality. Here again we must put aside an anthropological dualism that is utterly alien to Pauline theology. Paul is dealing with the human person in its entirety: it is the whole person that is set free "from the law of sin and death'' (Rom. 8:2) and laid hold of by ''the power of God'' (2 Cor. 6:7; cf. 1 Cor. 2:4 and Gal. 5:18).

God Is Spirit

In the final analysis, the power of God *is* God. That which dwells in us is the Spirit of God (Rom. 8:9), the Spirit of Christ (ibid.). In speaking of the distribution of charisms in the Christian community Paul treats as equivalents ''the same Spirit,'' ''the same Lord,'' and ''the same God'' (1 Cor. 12:4-6).[19]

If the human person may be described as spiritual in the second sense that I have distinguished, it is because of the action and presence of God and the Spirit in the deepest part of each of us. ''You are not in the flesh, you are in the Spirit, if the Spirit of God really dwells in you'' (Rom. 8:9). This dominion of the Spirit as source of life is so powerful, in Paul's view, that in many passages it is impossible to decide whether ''spirit'' refers to the human person under grace or to the Holy Spirit.[20] This difficulty is only the other side of the depth of the message itself about the intimate presence of the Spirit.

This presence, as I have said, always shows itself as an active power, a dynamism that leads to life (Rom. 8:6, 9). We saw earlier that the flesh is a death-dealing power (Rom. 8:6). The Spirit, on the contrary, is a life-giving power. There is not, however, a perfect antithesis. For, even though Paul at times personifies the flesh as a death-dealing power, we are here faced with something other than a personification: we are in the presence of a divine *person*, the Spirit. That is, we are in the presence of God as source of life.[21] God is Spirit and in Christ Jesus ''has set me free from the law of sin and death'' (Rom. 8:2), after condemning ''sin in the flesh'' (Rom. 8:3). The Spirit ''helps us in our weakness'' (Rom. 8:26) and rouses us to hope because ''there is . . . now no condemnation for those who are in Christ Jesus'' (Rom. 8:1).

The Resurrection Body

There is another central Pauline concept that we must study if we are to understand what this life according to the Spirit is. I am referring to the term *body* (*soma*), which, like *flesh* (*sarx*), trans-lates the Hebrew *basar* but with special overtones that need to be highlighted.[22] Once again we are dealing with a linked series of meanings that form a whole, although not an inflexible or mono-lithic whole.

The Body of Flesh

At times Paul uses the term "body" with a meaning very close to that of "flesh" in the first two senses I distinguished of this latter word when I analyzed it earlier.

The body as flesh designates the human being in its external aspect: "If I deliver my body to be burned, but have not love, I gain nothing" (1 Cor. 13:3); "Let not sin therefore reign in your mortal bodies" (Rom. 6:12; cf. 1 Cor. 9:27; 2 Cor. 4:10–11; Gal. 6:17). Paul can therefore speak of the "body of flesh" (Col. 1:22; 2:11) that is able to procreate (1 Cor. 7:4) and to die (Rom. 6:12; 2 Cor. 4:10–11). Its presence or absence in a place is the presence or absence of the entire person considered in its visible aspect: "For though absent in body I am present in spirit" (1 Cor. 5:3); "Though I am absent in body, yet I am with you in spirit" (Col. 2:5).[23]

Indeed, the body is not something the human person *has*, but something it *is*.[24] The "sin against the body" (1 Cor. 6:18) is prob-ably a sin against the whole person as a being called to a different destiny. But, as in the case of the flesh, the person insofar as it is body is subject to a certain weakness and can be ensnared by sin and by the death-dealing power that is the flesh (in one sense of this last term). It is possible, therefore, to speak of "the body of sin" (Rom. 6:6) that by its "works" (Rom. 8:13) leads the person to death: "Who will deliver me from this body of death?" (Rom. 7:24). At this point the body seems to be identified with the flesh of sin, but the identification is not complete.

The body is rather to be regarded as the field on which the flesh as death-dealing power operates, but where at the same time the Spirit, the power that gives life, is also active. For this reason Paul draws up a list of sins "according to the flesh" but not "accord-ing to the body." The body (the human person as body), as we shall see below, is the human organism and as such cannot but be located within the economy of salvation. The body therefore possesses the possibility of living according to the Spirit.[25]

In this context it is important to keep in mind one further aspect of the meaning of "body." In speaking of the flesh as a name for the human person ("all flesh") I said that it connoted human solidarity. The reference is to that collective outlook that is characteristic of the biblical mind-set. The same holds for "body." This word likewise implies a dimension of union among human beings.[26] St. Paul will use this connotation as a basis for speaking of the church as the body of Christ.

The Spiritual Body

On various occasions Paul refers to the possibility that the human person even as body can live a life according to the Spirit.

He tells us, for example, to the surprise of those who totally equate flesh and body, that the body can be spiritual: "It is sown a physical body, it is raised a spiritual body. If there is a physical body, there is also a spiritual body" (1 Cor. 15:44). "Spiritual body" is a strong but not an isolated expression. In another passage of the same Letter Paul says that "the body is not meant for immorality, but for the Lord, and the Lord for the body" (1 Cor. 6:13). This double relatedness brings out the dignity of the body and does so all the more cogently when we remember that it is formulated by opposition to what had been said in the first part of the same verse: "Food is meant for the stomach, and the stomach for food." Stomach or "belly," as we saw, means the flesh. The flesh is corruptible; the body, on the other hand, bears within it a germ of incorruptibility; it exists for the Lord and will therefore be raised up. "God raised the Lord and will also raise us up by his power" (1 Cor. 6:14).

The "spiritual body" or "body for the Lord" is not something mysterious or impalpable that can exist only after death. It is an already present reality, provided that by the power of baptism we live even now the resurrection of the Lord and are journeying toward the fulness of a life we already possess in an inchoative way. "We were buried therefore with him by baptism into death, so that as Christ was raised from the dead by the glory of the

Father, we too might walk in newness of life" (Rom. 6:5).

The Lord's power lays hold of us in our present existence: "With full courage now as always Christ will be honored in my body, whether by life or by death" (Phil. 1:20). Thus the power of God "will change our lowly body to be like his glorious body, by the power which enables him even to subject all things to himself" (Phil. 3:21).

We are in the presence here of a transformation of the entire human being, inasmuch as we already know that "body" refers to this entirety. A "spiritual body" is one belonging to a person who "walks according to the Spirit," but it emphasizes the corporeal, material aspect of the human being involved in this process. This manner of speaking brings out once again the difference between the flesh as a power that leads to death and the body as capable of living a definitive kind of life.

This spiritual potential that the body has permits Paul to say of it that it is a temple of the Spirit: "Do you not know that your body is a temple of the Holy Spirit within you, which you have from God? You are not your own" (1 Cor. 6:19). You belong to God who is present in your bodies as in his temple. Another statement, no less well known than the one just cited, conveys the same idea: "I appeal to you therefore, brethren, by the mercies of God, to present your bodies as a living sacrifice, holy and acceptable to God, which is your spiritual worship" (Rom. 12:1). In the spiritual worship proper to the Christian communities, the person—here designated by the body—offers its life as a holy sacrifice to God. Here once again the dignity of the body is underscored.

It is in the light of the resurrection of Christ that Paul views the difference between flesh and body; in so doing he distances himself from the perspective adopted in the Old Testament.[27] The human person can become subject to the flesh as death-dealing power, and then we are faced with the "body of sin" and "body of death." But the person can also be under the dominion of the Spirit, the power that gives life; then "the sinful body" will be "destroyed" (Rom. 6:6), because "he who raised Christ Jesus from the dead will give life to your mortal bodies also through his Spirit who dwells in you" (Rom. 8:11). We are dealing then with "the spiritual body."[28]

This new life comes by way of a liberation, the "redemption of our bodies'' (Rom. 8:23). It is a redemption from death—the death that gets its sting from sin and its power from the law (1 Cor. 15:56). Death, sin, and law embody the power of the flesh: ''While we were living in the flesh, our sinful passions, aroused by the law, were at work in our members to bear fruit for death'' (Rom. 7:5). From this enslavement we have been freed ''through the body of Christ'' (Rom. 7:4), who died and was raised up. It has been granted to us, therefore, to live under the dominion of the Spirit who is *life* (''The Spirit is life because of justice'': Rom. 8:10, literal), *grace* (''Sin will have no dominion over you, since you are not under law but under grace'': Rom. 6:14), and *freedom* (''Where the Spirit of the Lord is, there is freedom'': 2 Cor. 3:17).

Precisely because of this dialectic of *death/life* Paul's theology of the body becomes the key to an understanding of Christian existence.[29] The body that has been freed from the forces of death will lead a life in the Spirit. ''Flesh and blood cannot inherit the kingdom of God'' (1 Cor. 15:50), but the liberated body can.[30]

The Body of Christ

The idea of body finds its supreme and most original use in Pauline theology when it is employed in speaking of Christ and our incorporation into him. The theme is a very extensive one, and I shall here be touching on only the few aspects that are connected with my theme in these pages.

Death has been overcome in the body of Christ Jesus that was nailed to the cross, whereas life proclaims its final victory in the risen body of the Lord. ''For we know that Christ being raised from the dead will never die again; death no longer has dominion over him'' (Rom. 6:9). Christians are members of this dead and risen body, and they are such by reason of their own bodies: ''Do you not know that your bodies are members of Christ?'' (1 Cor. 6:15).

This approach leads Paul to use the word body in a supra-individual perspective. Body is a factor in solidarity,[31] and the body of Christ is the entire Christian community: ''You are the body of Christ and individually members of it'' (1 Cor. 12:27). This totality, which is the church, has Christ for its head: God "has made him the head over all things for the church, which is his body, the fulness (*pleroma*) of him who fills all in all" (Eph. 1:22-23). Within this one whole there are different functions: "As in one body we have many members, and all the members do not have the same function, so we, though many, are one body in Christ, and individually members one of another" (Rom. 12: 4-5).

Readers often regard this theology of the church as simply a beautiful metaphor. However, we must, shocking though this idea may be, see through to the realism that characterizes the Pauline approach. He is speaking of the real body of Christ,[32] which he looks upon as an extension of the incarnation.[33] I simply emphasize this point without going into it in detail.

The journey from death to life "through the body of Christ" (Rom. 7:4) is one that every Christian must make. It is an ongoing process for each Christian life and for the community as a whole. Because they are bodies, both individual and community are subject to the powers of death and life. Paul says: "We are afflicted in every way . . . always carrying in the body the death of Jesus, so that the life of Jesus may also be manifested in our bodies"; and the passage continues: "for while we live we are always being given up to death for Jesus' sake, so that the life of Jesus may be manifested in our mortal flesh" (2 Cor. 4:10-11). Because of this, the church, as body of Christ, will be characterized by a reciprocal giving and receiving in relation to these forces of death and life: "So death is at work in us, but life in you" (ibid., v. 12).

It hardly needs saying that in thus listing various meanings of the words "flesh," "spirit," and "body," I am not claiming to list all their possible meanings or combinations in Paul's use of them. For at times he will call into play all the different nuances in the gamut of meanings that I have discussed (along with other less important ones that I have not mentioned for fear of unduly complicating the subject). What I have sought to emphasize is the profound unity that pervades these series of meanings, as well as the horizon within which they are located. One sphere bears the mark of *death* (sin and the law), the other of *life* (grace and freedom).[34]

Human life unfolds within an option for death or an option for life. Deuteronomy expounds this point with all desirable clarity in a much cited passage: "I have set before you this day life and good, death and evil" (30:15). Paul adopts this same perspective in a very vigorous way and turns it into the focus of Christian spirituality. To walk according to the Spirit is to reject death (selfishness, contempt for others, covetousness, idolatry) and choose life (love, peace, justice). To renounce the flesh and live according to the Spirit is to be at the service of God and others. This service is offered with the conviction that the forces of death will not have the final word in history, because we know that "in all these things we are more than conquerors through him who loved us" (Rom. 8:37). Nothing, and no one, "will be able to separate us from the love of God in Christ Jesus our Lord" (v.38).[35]

We have to decide between death and life—that is, between flesh and spirit.[36] The choice is not between body and soul; nothing could be further from the thinking of Paul who establishes instead a religious (and not a philosophical) opposition between flesh and spirit. He is always dealing with the human person as a whole. It is the whole person who must know how to choose the Spirit and life. In making this choice we have on our side the power of love—the Spirit—which is more interior to us than we are to ourselves, as Augustine of Hippo puts it.

A spirituality, which is a way of being a Christian, has as its foundation an advance through death, sin, and slavery, in accordance with the Spirit, who is the life-giving power that sets the human person free. To be a Christian is to be free of all external coercion: "Where the Spirit of the Lord is, there is freedom" (2 Cor. 3:17), a freedom put at the service of God and neighbor.[37] To reject the power of the flesh does not mean to have contempt for the body. On the contrary, Christian spirituality consists in *embracing the liberated body* and thus being able both to pray "Abba, Father!" and to enter into a comradely communion with others.[38]

It is important not to miss the profound continuity of the entire process. The resurrected body of the Lord is the body of flesh and the crucified body that were the medium of his presence in history.[39] We are in the same situation through our belonging to the body of Christ. Our own bodies, freed from the flesh with its death-dealing power, become spiritual and a means of life and solidarity.

This necessarily corporeal and communal new existence continues to be subject to the powers of death and life; during its historical course it is not yet definitively confirmed in grace, but is called to make progress, although retrogression is not impossible. Nonetheless, in making our decision we know that "the Spirit helps us in our weakness" (Rom. 8:26).

Life according to the Spirit is therefore not an existence at the level of the soul and in opposition to or apart from the body; it is an existence *in accord with life*, love, peace, and justice (the great values of the reign of God) and *against death*. Such is the spiritual life of Christians, "heirs of God and fellow heirs with Christ" (Rom. 8:17), because "all who are led by the Spirit of God are sons of God" (Rom. 8:14). The fact that God is a father, the gift of filiation, the fellowship that filiation demands—these constitute "the mystery which was kept secret for long ages but is now disclosed" (Rom. 16:25-26) in the death and resurrection of Jesus Christ.

This gift accounts for the fact that "if, because of one man's trespass, death reigned through that one man, much more will those who receive the abundance of grace and the free gift of righteousness reign in life through the one man Jesus Christ" (Rom. 5:17).

5

A PEOPLE IN SEARCH OF GOD

Encounter with the Lord is the point of departure for a life according to the Spirit. This life finds expression in a journey in search of God. This is what Paul calls "a more excellent way" (*kath hyperbolen hodon*; 1 Cor. 12:31); it consists in the practice of the love that brings us "face to face" with God (1 Cor. 13:12).

We are talking here about the journey of an entire people and not of isolated individuals. The paradigmatic experience of the Jewish people in its exodus to the promised land has inspired many spiritual writers with images for describing—and understanding—their own experiences. The Book of Acts lends further support to this approach by speaking of the Christian manner of life simply as "the way."

Christianity is the way by which the Spirit leads the new "messianic people," the church, through history. This historical journey is a collective one because an entire community accomplishes it. It has a comprehensive character also inasmuch as every aspect of human existence is caught up in the process. In the spiritual tradition we find many examples of how these biblical perspectives influence the understanding of the spiritual journey to God. The different courses undertaken by Christians throughout history in their following of Jesus lead, moreover, to a reorganization and new synthesis of the main focuses of the gospel, in accordance with the demands of a given age.

The Spirituality of a People

The exodus of the Jewish people and the way undertaken by the early church are radical experiences and as such the source of many others in the course of the Jewish-Christian tradition.

Learning to be Free

The exodus was the foundational experience of the Jewish people.[1] It involved a departure from a situation of slavery, exploitation, and destitution in Egypt, a foreign country, and a passage, via a multifaceted process of liberation, into freedom, justice, and the possession of a land of their own, the promised land:

> And God said to Moses, "I am the Lord. I appeared to Abraham, to Isaac, and to Jacob, as God Almighty [*El Shaddai*], but by my name the Lord [*Yahweh*] I did not make myself known to them. I also established my covenant with them, to give them the land of Canaan, the land in which they dwelt as sojourners. Moreover I have heard the groaning of the people of Israel whom the Egyptians hold in bondage and I have remembered my covenant. Say therefore to the people of Israel, 'I am the Lord, and I will bring you out from under the burdens of the Egyptians, and I will deliver you from their bondage, and I will redeem you with an outstretched arm and with great acts of judgment, and I will take you for my people, and I will be your God; and you shall know that I am the Lord your God, who has brought you out from under the burdens of the Egyptians. And I will bring you into the land which I swore to give to Abraham, to Isaac, and to Jacob; I will give it to you for a possession. I am the Lord' " [Exod. 6:2–8].

SEEKING GOD. The departure from Egypt meant a breaking away from death (for that is what enslavement and need mean) in order to go forth and meet Yahweh and become the people of Yahweh.[2] On this journey of liberation—and not apart from it—

the people sought God. That search was the ultimate meaning of the entire process.

There was here a break, led by a liberator whom Yahweh had called, from a deplorable situation of slavery, to which, nonetheless, the people remained bound by subtle and cowardly complicities. The country they were leaving was a foreign one, but the land there was rich. "For the land which you are entering to take possession of it is not like the land of Egypt, from which you have come; where you sowed your seed and watered it with your feet, like a garden of vegetables" (Deut. 11:10).

For this very reason the break was not accomplished once and for all. It was rather an ongoing process that entailed a struggle against all the forces urging a return to the former state of things (the attraction of "the fleshpots of Egypt"). To celebrate the memory of that departure (that going out or ex-odus, a word derived from the Greek *hodos*, "way") was to celebrate the love of God and to confirm once again the choice that had been made.

As a matter of fact, the feast of passover recalled the purpose of the departure: "Thus says the Lord, the God of Israel, 'Let my people go, that they may hold a feast to me in the wilderness' " (Exod. 5:1). The realization of the liberating love of Yahweh had been present from the beginning of the process. At the same time, when this festival of liberation and life was celebrated outside the land of enslavement and death, it served as a means of learning freedom during the crossing of the wilderness and its solitude. The full experience of that freedom was to come in the communion of the promised land.[3]

THAT THEY MIGHT KNOW THE LORD. The people that had left Egypt set out on a journey through the wilderness. It was a lengthy pilgrimage, lasting forty years according to the Bible. It was a time of trial and of a deepening of the knowledge of Yahweh who had liberated the Jewish people from slavery. That is why the prophets later called upon them to keep that journey constantly in mind and to draw conclusions from it for their current life.

A basic question would be raised: Why so lengthy a route? Why so long a time for a journey over what was really a short distance? Without dwelling on historical details the biblical writers adopt a perspective dictated by faith, and they find the answer to that question in the deeper meaning of the journey itself:

> You shall remember all the way which the Lord your God has led you these forty years in the wilderness, that he might humble you, testing you to know what was in your heart, whether you would keep his commandments, or not. And he humbled you and let you hunger and fed you with manna, which you did not know, nor did your fathers know; that he might make you know that man does not live by bread alone, but that man lives by everything that proceeds out of the mouth of the Lord. Your clothing did not wear out upon you, and your foot did not swell, these forty years. Know then in your heart that, as a man disciplines his son, the Lord your God disciplines you. So you shall keep the commandments of the Lord your God, by walking in his ways and fearing him [Deut. 8:2–6].

The important thing here is the mutual knowledge of Yahweh and the people, which is compared to that between father and son. The time in the wilderness was a time of testing that enabled Yahweh to "learn the profound intentions" of the people in its everyday life, before entering the promised land. But at the same time the wilderness period was also an opportunity for the revelation of Yahweh's love for the Israelites, by showing them concern for the material side of their life ("Your clothing did not wear out upon you, and your foot did not swell") and by teaching them that they must feed upon Yahweh's word and not only on bread. In this way the Israelites would come "to know their Lord and God." This would in turn enable them to observe God's commandments and follow God's ways. Growth in this reciprocal knowledge included growth in mutual love, for, as we know, the biblical word "know" has the connotation of intimacy and affectivity. Such, then, is the deeper meaning of the journey through the wilderness; it gave unity and direction to what might otherwise seem simply dispersion and wandering.[4]

In this "twofold apprenticeship" Israel had to learn new ways. Its journey was through the wilderness where no pathways had been carved out in advance. There the footprints of a traveler are soon effaced by wind and sand. In a wilderness or desert we neither find nor leave any trail. Wayfarers must decide on their own path with complete freedom. The Israelites are exhorted by the prophets to prepare a way for Yahweh to meet them: "In the wilderness prepare the way of the Lord, make straight in the desert a highway for our God" (Isa. 40:3, cited in Matt. 3:3 and Mark 1:3). On its journey to the promised land the people that had been liberated from slavery and forced labor learned to be free while turning itself into a nation.

This experience of freedom was to leave its impress on the life and spirituality of Israel. It was on the basis of that experience that Israel understood itself as a people and was proud of it. This comes out clearly in a conversation between Jesus and "the Jews" recorded in the Gospel of John. The Jews respond to Jesus' call to freedom by saying:

"We are descendants of Abraham, and have never been in bondage to any one. How is it that you say, 'You will be made free'?" Jesus answered them, "Truly, truly, I say to you, every one who commits sin is a slave to sin. The slave does not continue in the house for ever; the son continues for ever. So if the Son makes you free, you will be free indeed" [John 8:33–36].

As the Jews saw it, to be *Jewish* meant that they were free. Jesus, however, invites them to understand freedom in a deeper way: to be *sons and daughters*—to be adopted offspring of God—is to be truly free. The slave does not remain in the house of the Father; slaves are not offspring.

It is in the terrible solitude of the wilderness that the Israelites exercise their creativity in opening up new ways. Fears assail them (Ps. 107:5), and there are many threats to their lives. The wandering in the desert meant poverty and scarcity imposed by the inhospitable land they were traversing. They had given up their homes only in the hope for something better. This is why they are repeatedly tempted to regress, to turn back: "And they said to one another, 'Let us choose a captain, and go back to Egypt' " (Num. 14:4). This would have meant a return to slavery out of fear of a difficult and demanding freedom. Thus it was amid advances and regressions that the journey to the promised land was accomplished.

YOU WOULD NOT SEEK ME IF YOU HAD NOT ALREADY FOUND ME. The Jewish people left Egypt ("the house of bondage": Deut. 8:14) in order to enter the promised land and not in order to keep on wandering in the wilderness:

> For the Lord your God is bringing you into a good land, a land of brooks of water, of fountains and springs, flowing forth in valleys and hills, a land of wheat and barley, of vines and fig trees and pomegranates, a land of olive trees and honey, a land in which you will eat bread without scarcity, in which you will lack nothing, a land whose stones are iron, and out of whose hills you can dig copper. And you shall eat and be full, and you shall bless the Lord your God for the good land he has given you [Deut. 8:7–10].[5]

The Jewish people set out in quest of an encounter with God. But in a way this encounter was already a reality at the beginning of the journey. Even when the Israelites were still in Egypt, Yahweh expressed close and sympathetic awareness of their situation: "I have seen the affliction of my people who are in Egypt, and have heard their cry because of their taskmasters; I know their sufferings, and I have come down to deliver them out of the hand of the Egyptians, and to bring them up out of that land to a good and broad land, a land flowing with milk and honey" (Exod. 3:7–8). Yahweh commissioned Moses and Aaron to tell the people that "the Lord, the God of the Hebrews, has met with us" (Exod. 3:18). The first encounter prefigured a much greater expansion of communion.

It was precisely because of this anticipated encounter with God that the movement of quest could begin, in accord with the well-known words of Augustine: "You would not seek me if you had not already found me." The search for union with the Lord governs the entire process of liberation and constitutes the very heart of this spiritual experience of an entire people.

The promised land is not simply a new country; it is also the gift of a radically different situation:

> For behold, I create new heavens
>   and a new earth;
> and the former things shall not be remembered
>   or come into mind.
> But be glad and rejoice for ever
>   in that which I create;
> for behold, I create Jerusalem a rejoicing,
>   and her people a joy.
> I will rejoice in Jerusalem,
>   and be glad in my people;
> no more shall be heard in it the sound of weeping
>   and the cry of distress.
> No more shall there be in it
>   an infant that lives but a few days,
>   or an old man who does not fill out his days,
> for the child shall die a hundred years old,
>   and the sinner a hundred years old shall be ac-
>   cursed.
> They shall build houses and inhabit them;
>   they shall plant vineyards and eat their fruit.
> They shall not build and another inhabit;
>   they shall not plant and another eat;
> for like the days of a tree shall the days of my
>   people be,
>   and my chosen shall long enjoy the work of
>   their hands.
> They shall not labor in vain,
>   or bear children for calamity;
> for they shall be the offspring of the blessed of
>   the Lord,
>   and their children with them [Isa. 65:17-23].

This is the new situation wherein joy will take root in the fulfilled promise that justice would be established.

This land in which there will be no exploitation and no need is, in the final analysis, an unmerited gift of the Lord and the pledge of commitment to the people with whom the Lord is establishing a covenant: "You shall be my people, and I will be your God." This gift sets everything in motion and leaves its imprint on the process from the beginning. Yahweh is sole owner of the earth: "All the earth is mine" (Exod. 19:5), and the purpose of the earth is to give life to all.[6] This is why any unjust appropriation of land by an individual is contrary to God's will: "Woe to those who join house to house, who add field to field, until there is no more room, and you are made to dwell alone in the midst of the land. The Lord of hosts has sworn in my hearing: 'Surely many houses shall be made desolate, large and beautiful houses, without inhabitant' " (Isa. 5:8-9). "To dwell alone" implies, to some extent, the death of those for whom "there is no more room."

But in the final analysis possession of the land ought to be an occasion for remembering Yahweh—that is, for keeping in mind Yahweh's love and demands:

Take heed lest you forget the Lord your God, by not keeping his commandments and his ordinances and his statutes, which I command you this day: lest, when you have eaten and are full, and have built goodly houses and live in them, and when your herds and flocks multiply, and your silver and gold is multiplied, and all that you have is multiplied, then your heart be lifted up, and you forget the Lord your God who brought you out of the land of Egypt, out of the house of bondage [Deut. 8:11-14].

Life in the promised land should be a life lived in the presence of God and marked by fulfillment of the requirements of justice toward others. The land is the place and occasion for communion with God and communion among human beings. For this land is the manifestation of Yahweh's fidelity: it is "a land which the Lord your God cares for; the eyes of the Lord your God are always upon it, from the beginning of the year to the end of the year" (Deut. 11:12). It should also be a place where God's commandments are observed. All this is included in the theme of the promised land.

The New Way

After the experience of the exodus, "walking in the ways of the Lord" (Ps. 128:1) became a recurring theme in Israelite spirituality. It is taken up again with intensity and originality in the Acts of the Apostles, where the perspective is always the life of an entire people.

A LIFESTYLE. A superficial reading of Paul might make the reader think that the life according to the Spirit that he sets before us (we reviewed it above) is something entirely personal and even insular. In fact, however, the importance that the theology of the body of Christ has in Paul's message invalidates this interpretation, for it brings out the social dimensions of the process. But if there were still any doubt, the approach taken by the Book of Acts makes everything clear. This is especially important because in this approach the connection with Paul's own experience is rendered explicit.

Acts is the only book of the New Testament that calls Christianity *the way* (*hodos*); in most of its uses the term stands alone, without qualifiers. The first time we meet it is in the account of the conversion of Saul of Tarsus:

> But Saul, still breathing threats and murder against the disciples of the Lord, went to the high priest and asked him for letters to the synagogues at Damascus, so that if he found any belonging to the Way, men or women, he might bring them bound to Jerusalem. Now as he journeyed he approached Damascus, and suddenly a light from heaven flashed about him. And he fell to the ground and heard a voice saying to him, "Saul, Saul, why do you persecute me?" And he said, "Who are you, Lord?" And he said, "I am Jesus, whom you are persecuting" [Acts 9:1-5].

This text is of major importance, and it connects the expression "the way," which is original with Acts, to the spiritual experience of Paul. The expression will be repeated in a second version of his conversion, one that is put this time in the mouth of Paul himself: "I persecuted this Way to the death, binding and delivering to prison both men and women" (Acts 22:4). Further on in the latter passage the point is made once again that this persecution was a persecution of Jesus himself: "I fell to the ground and heard a voice saying to me, 'Saul, Saul, why do you persecute me? And I answered, 'Who are you, Lord?' And he said to me, 'I am Jesus of Nazareth, whom you are persecuting' '' (22:7-8; cf. 26:9).

The word "way" is applied to Christians themselves; it is also opposed to the accusation of sectarianism that their enemies leveled against them. Thus in a defense that Paul makes before Felix the governor, he says: "This I admit to you, that according to the Way, which they call a sect, I worship the God of my fathers, believing everything laid down by the law or written in the prophets" (24:14; see also 19:9, 23; 24:22). In three instances "way" is more closely defined: "the way of salvation" (Acts 16:17), "the way of the Lord" (18:25), and "the way of God" (18:26).

What is the meaning of the term? According to some, "way" designates Christians themselves, not a lifestyle.[7] According to others, "way" refers chiefly to Christian teaching.[8] Nonetheless, everything indicates that a sound interpretation requires a global and synthetic perspective.

In point of fact, Christians are characterized by a certain behavior, a manner of life. This manner of life singles out the Christian community in the Jewish and pagan world in which it lives and gives its witness. Its conduct reflects at once a manner of thinking and a manner of acting—in short, a way of life; nothing falls outside this way.[9] The meaning of the Hebrew word for "way" lays emphasis on an ethical approach that extends to the whole of life: "You shall teach them the statutes and the decisions, and make them know the way (*derek*) in which they must walk and what they must do" (Exod. 18:20).[10]

It is in this sense that Paul uses the term: "Therefore I sent to you Timothy, my beloved and faithful child in the Lord, to remind you of my conduct (*hodos*) in Christ, as I teach them everywhere in every church" (1 Cor. 4:17). To follow the *way* is to practice a certain *conduct*; the same Greek word is used for both ideas. What is meant is conduct in the service of God.[11] It is a manner of life that is taught through witness and that can in turn be followed by others: "I urge you, then, be imitators of me," says Paul in the verse immediately preceding the ones just cited.

FREEDOM AND LOVE. The conduct to be observed is a way that Paul presents in this same letter as superior to any other. After speaking of the importance and advantages of the various charisms present in the body of Christ, Paul writes: "But earnestly desire the higher gifts. And I will show a still more excellent way [*kath' huperbolen hodon*]" (1 Cor. 12:31). These words are followed by the well-known hymn to love that occupies the whole of chapter 13. For the way in question is in fact the way of love that shapes the whole of Christian life because love "bears all things, believes all things, hopes all things, endures all things. Love never ends" (vv. 7–8). The charisms will disappear, and even faith and hope will cease to be necessary, because we shall see God "face to face." Only love will remain, the love that, as we already know, is the supreme fruit of the Spirit.

The way in question, the way that seals the witness given by the Christian community, is the way of the Spirit—which is to say, the way of love that expresses itself in deeds. It is the way of salvation, the way of the Lord, the way of God. Paul calls this way "the law of the Spirit of life in Christ Jesus," which has set us free "from the law of sin and death" (Rom. 8:2), because "if you are led by the Spirit you are not under the law" (Gal. 5:18).[12] We live in the regime of grace: "you are not under the law but under grace" (Rom. 6:14), and of freedom: "for freedom Christ has set us free; stand fast therefore, and do not submit again to a yoke of slavery (*douleias*)" (Gal. 5:1).

To follow the way is to live in Christ the Lord (Col. 2:6). For the Christian way is not directed by an external law; it is identified with a person, with Jesus,[13] the free man.[14] Paul's conversion experience, which we recalled just above, bears witness to this identification. Everyone agrees that that experience was the starting point for his theology of the body of Christ.

The Christian way is the way of freedom, and to freedom we have been called (Gal. 5:13).[15] This is an already familiar theme. But we are also aware that this freedom is not for personal satisfaction and use, and that it is not complete unless it is exercised in the framework of the practice of love: "Only do not use your freedom as an opportunity for the flesh (*sarx*), but through love be servants [*douleuete*: literally, 'be slaves'] of one another" (Gal. 5:13). These two paradoxical statements underscore the thought of the Apostle. Freedom is always presented as the work of the Spirit and something positive; here the writer forces his terms somewhat and speaks of freedom as possibly being used to serve the death-dealing power of the flesh. Secondly, slavery, which is a term used for a situation contrary to the spirit of filiation and freedom, is here used of the comradely service that the children of God should offer to one another. Paul's approach here brings out even more cogently the primacy of love in the practice of freedom. It is this primacy that enables Augustine to say in a well-known and daring statement: "Love; then do what you want."

One final point, as I end these considerations on what the Book of Acts calls "the Way." The pages of Acts tell us of the road traveled and the testimony given by the first Christian community. In the first twelve chapters the Spirit is mentioned thirty-seven times. It is under the sign of the Spirit that the church, the "messianic people" and (in Paul's phrase) the "body of Christ," travels its way. As in the case of the Jewish people (see the previous section), so here the journey is a collective undertaking in which the Spirit of God is the moving force.[16] It is an undertaking in which a people learns to live its freedom in the service of love. That precisely is its spirituality, its "walking according to the Spirit" (Rom. 8:4).

A Manner of Being a Christian

The biblical models provided by the exodus and the early church have left their mark on Christian experience and reflection as far as the path to be followed in the search for God is concerned. They have inspired the itineraries of the great mystics, as well as those followed by the Christian people as a whole. It will be worth our while to examine some testimonies in this area, keeping in mind that they are offered only as examples. Nor may we forget that each experience reshapes the route in its own way, sets up a different hierarchy of values, and reorganizes the major foci of Christian life in terms of certain basic intuitions.

The Spiritual Path

St. John of the Cross presents the passage from flesh to Spirit, the "former" person to the "new," death to life, sin to the grace

of communion with God and others, as an advancing series of
three nights or three parts of one night. "These three nights pass
through the soul, or better, the soul passes through them in order
to reach divine union with God."[17] The soul—that is, Christians
launched on the search for God—must pass through these nights.
The term "night" is used "because . . . the soul journeys in darkness as though by night."[18] It is a road traveled in darkness, a
"frightful night"[19] that John of the Cross will examine in subtle
detail on the basis of his own experience.

THE DEPARTURE. The point of departure for the spiritual journey is a break, a going forth. That constitutes the first night: "The
first has to do with the point of departure, because the individual
must deprive himself of his appetite for worldly possessions. This
denial and privation is like a night for all his senses."[20] The first
stanza reads:

> One dark night,
> Fired with love's urgent longings
> —Ah, the sheer grace!—
> I went out unseen,
> My house being now stilled.[21]

John of the Cross explains what it is the soul goes out from:
"The soul sings in this first stanza of its good luck and the grace it
had in departing from its inordinate appetites and imperfec-
tions."[22] There is a break with what Paul speaks of as the flesh,
whose end, we know, is death.

The Carmelite mystic continues: "In this stanza the soul desires
to declare in summary fashion that it departed on a dark night,
attracted by God and enkindled with love for him alone."[23] As in
the case of the Jewish people, the departure is a manifestation of
the liberating action of God ("the Lord brought us out . . . by his
mighty hand" [Deut. 6:22]). Here as there the ultimate motivat-
ing force in the process is the love of God.

This departure presupposes a battle or even a war, as John of
the Cross calls it: "Until slumber comes to the appetites through
the mortification of sensuality, and until this very sensuality is
stilled in such a way that the appetites do not war against the
spirit, the soul will not walk out to genuine freedom, to the enjoy-

ment of union with its Beloved.''[24] The stillness that makes it possible for the soul to go forth is the result of a victory over itself. This is the classic spiritual struggle to which the spiritual writers bear witness. Only then is the soul in a condition to live the freedom that is characteristic of life in accordance with the Spirit. The fulness of freedom is found in union with God.

A VENTURE OF FAITH. Abraham's departure at the bidding of God—"Go from your country and your kindred and your father's house to the land that I will show you" (Gen. 12:1)—is always regarded in the Bible as the prototype of faith. Hebrews 11 supplies us with the well-known list of those who journeyed in faith. The road to God is a venture of faith.

The second night is "the road along which a person travels to this union. Now this road is faith, and for the intellect faith is also like a dark night.''[25] The second stanza speaks of this night:

> In darkness, and secure,
> By the secret ladder, disguised,
> —Ah, the sheer grace!—
> In darkness and concealment,
> My house being now all stilled.

The Carmelite comments: "The soul . . . affirms that it departed 'in darkness, and secure.' For anyone fortunate enough to possess the ability to journey in the obscurity of faith, as a blind man with his guide, and depart from all natural phantasms and intellectual reasonings, walks securely.''[26] Thanks to faith, it is a secure journeying, despite the fact that it takes place in the depths of night, for this night is "darker" than the first; "accordingly it is compared to midnight, the innermost and darkest period of night.''[27] The journey is an unbroken and demanding process, because "not to go forward on this road is to turn back, and not to gain ground is to lose.''[28]

Like the Jewish people in the wilderness, one traveling this road travels in the greatest solitude. Solitude, but not selfish withdrawal, is a central factor in every experience of God, for it is in the wilderness that God speaks to us: "I will allure her, and bring her into the wilderness, and speak tenderly to her" (Hos. 2:14). Solitude thus understood has nothing to do with individualism.

Nor is solitude opposed to communion; on the contrary, it prepares us for communion and creates authentic dispositions for it. Without the experience of solitude there is no communion, nor is there any union with God or any genuine sharing with others. John of the Cross sings of solitude:

> She lived in solitude,
> And now in solitude has built her nest;
> And in solitude he guides her,
> He alone, who also bears
> In solitude the wound of love.[29]

Commenting elsewhere on the secrecy of this journey of faith, John again takes over the biblical theme of the wilderness:

> This mystical wisdom will occasionally so engulf a person in its secret abyss that he will have the keen awareness of being brought into a place far removed from every creature. He will accordingly feel that he has been led into a remarkably deep and vast wilderness, unattainable by any human creature, into an immense, unbounded desert, the more delightful, savorous, and loving, the deeper, vaster, and more solitary it is.[30]

There is no route already marked out in this "immense desert," this "deep and vast wilderness." Here, as on the sea, "paths . . . shall not be known."[31] The spiritual journey is marked by a constant creative freedom under the action of the Spirit. In the sketch of the ascent of Mount Carmel the three famous paths are indicated at the foot of the mountain: the mistaken one to the right, the imperfect one to the left, and the narrow one of perfection in the middle. But when this narrow path reaches the lower slope of the hill and is already close to the top where "only the honor and glory of God dwells," and when it has on both sides the gifts and fruits of the Spirit (according to Gal. 5:22), this highly significant sentence is to be found: "Here there is no longer any way, because for the just man there is no law."[32]

As we have seen, the spiritual path is characterized by freedom from all external coercion. That is the point St. John of the Cross

is making so beautifully when he tells us that no way is marked out
for the ascent to union with God. All the great mystics share that
same deep conviction. Thus in the Preamble to his *Constitutions*,
which regulate in detail—and with spiritual and psychological
insight—the life and apostolate of the Society of Jesus, Ignatius
of Loyola writes: "What helps most on our part toward this end
must be, more than any exterior constitution, the interior law of
charity and love which the Holy Spirit writes and engraves upon
hearts."[33]

THE PERIOD BEFORE THE DAWN. The soul departs in order to
enter: "The attainment of our goal demands that we never stop
on the road."[34] The goal of the journey is to be found in the third
night: "The third . . . pertains to the point of arrival, namely,
God. And God is also a dark night to man in this life."[35] An initial
state of union with God is attainable in this life. While the darkness remains, the light of day makes its presence known.

The third night or the third part of the night is "the period
before the dawn"—that is, it "approximates the light of day. The
darkness is not like that of midnight, since in this third period of
the night we approach the illumination of day. And this daylight
we compare to God. . . . This light is the principle of the perfect
union which follows after the third night."[36]

This union and the arrival at it is presented in the final stanza of
the *Ascent*:

> I abandoned and forgot myself,
> Laying my face on my Beloved;
> All things ceased; I went out from myself,
> Leaving my cares
> Forgotten among the lilies.[37]

"All things ceased": the final stage is equivalent to arrival in
the "land flowing with milk and honey," insofar as the entry is a
definitive one. The road reaches its goal, and without thinking
any longer of himself the traveler can rest "leaving his cares
forgotten among the lilies."

The paradigms of the exodus and of the nights of John of the
Cross throw light on each other. We must not be deceived by the

difference of tone. The historical and personal dimensions inter-
twine and enrich each other within a process that follows the same
basic pattern in both cases.

An All-Embracing Perspective

There is no aspect of human life that is unrelated to the following of Jesus.[38] The road passes through every dimension of our
existence, as we saw in the biblical models discussed earlier. A
spirituality is not restricted to the so-called religious aspects of
life: prayer and worship. It is not limited to one sector but is all-
embracing, because the whole of human life, personal and communal, is involved in the journey. A spirituality is a manner of life
that gives a profound unity to our prayer, thought, and action.

This comprehensiveness is due to the fact that the journey is
undertaken under the movement of the Spirit, and the Spirit, as
we know, "will guide us into all the truth" (John 16:13). This
truth gives shape to our life in its entirety and "makes us free"
(John 8:32). A spirituality is, in effect, the field in which freedom
is exercised—the full freedom that energizes and feeds our option
for life and against death. In addition, totality is demanded by
reciprocity. As Teresa of Avila says, "God does not give himself
entirely to us, unless we give ourselves entirely to God."[39]

At the same time, however, it is not enough to emphasize this
comprehensiveness, fundamental though it is. For a synthesis
may have a variety of starting points. This is precisely what we see
in the great spiritualities that the Christian community has
known. Each strives to encompass the various aspects of Christian life, and yet each differs from the others.

The reason for this diversity is that the nucleus around which a
spiritual way is built is not exactly the same in every case. Moreover, the starting point in each instance bears the mark of the
historical context in which the experience of encounter with the
Lord took place. The times and the needs of the poor and of the
church were not the same for Augustine of Hippo, Francis de
Sales, and Thérèse of Lisieux. Nor were the spiritual experiences
of these three individuals the same, yet in each instance the experience was such that it left a profound mark on the Christian community.[40]

A particular spirituality always represents a reorganizing of the fundamental foci of Christian life, on the basis of a central intuition or insight. The intuition is that of great men and women of the Spirit as they respond to the needs and demands of their age. Every spirituality is a way that is offered for the greater service of God and others: freedom to love. The difference between one spirituality and another is not the foci to which I have referred, for these are usually the same; the difference is in the new way of organizing them, the new synthesis that is elaborated.[41] And the newness in this area is due to the experience that gives rise to a spiritual way.[42]

The concrete forms taken by the crystalization of evangelical themes and requirements around a central insight may differ, but in every case the end result shows the comprehensiveness, the all-inclusiveness, that is characteristic of every great spirituality. There is a style of life that gives a distinctive personality to *one* manner of being a Christian. This manner is in fact a limited manner, for no spirituality can claim to be *the* way to be a Christian. It is simply one way among others.

As we saw in discussing the biblical models, "walking according to the Spirit" is an activity undertaken within a community, a people on the move.[43] This is a dimension of every spirituality, despite presentations that at times suggest that a spirituality is for a purely individual journey. When I say that the following of Jesus is a collective adventure I am, of course, not eliminating the personal dimension; on the contrary, I am giving it its authentic meaning as a response to the con-vocation of the Father. In God we shall find that "whole truth" to which the inbreathing of the Spirit is leading us in the following of Christ.

PART THREE

Free to Love

Encounter with the Lord, a life according to the Spirit, a wayfaring that embraces all aspects of life and is done in community: these are dimensions of every journeying in search of God.

In this process the way is carved out as we go, because no previously traced route exists. Spirituality, as I have said repeatedly, is the area of the Spirit's action; it is therefore characterized by freedom. To quench the Spirit (1 Thess. 5:19) is to do away with the fruit of the Spirit: love and those actions in relation to God and neighbor in which love finds expression; with regard to these "there is no law" (Gal. 5:23). Law in this context is external coercion and, as such, is associated with the flesh and death.

St. James can therefore say: "So speak and so act as those who are to be judged under *the law of liberty*" (James 2:12). The law of freedom, the law of the Spirit, is the law by which will be judged the works without which faith is dead (James 2:14, 26). We know too that, according to the Letter of James, these works are above all those done for the "poor in the world" whom God has chosen as "heirs of the kingdom which he has promised to those who love him" (2:5).

Jesus gives us an example of freedom as a distinguishing trait of a life in the service of others. This service is expressed in and acquires its meaning from the way in which Jesus controls the surrender of his own life: "No one takes it [my life] from me, but I lay it down of my own accord" (John 10:18). This is the attitude of one who comes to decisions without being influenced by external pressures, and who makes these decisions out of love for others. Jesus *freely* decides to give his life in *solidarity* with those who are under the power of death. Freedom exercised within a communion of life: such is the meaning of Christian freedom, such is the context for its full development.[1]

In part 1 I analyzed certain passages of Paul (e.g., Gal. 5:1 and 13). It was these texts that gave rise to the familiar distinction, taken over by St. Thomas Aquinas among others, between freedom *from* and freedom *for*. "Freedom from" refers to freedom from sin, from selfishness, from injustice, from need; all these are conditions that call for a liberation. "Freedom for" states the purpose of the freedom acquired: freedom for love, for communion; the attainment of love and communion is the final stage in liberation. "Free to love": this phrase, inspired by Paul (another text in the same line is that of 1 Cor. 9:19: "though I am free from all men, I have made myself a slave to all [*edoulosa*]"), expresses the full meaning of the process of liberation to which many Latin American Christians are committed.[2] In the final analysis, to set free is to give life[3]—communion with God and with others—or, to use the language of Puebla, liberation for communion and participation.[4]

In this context of the struggle for liberation for the sake of love and justice, a distinctive way of following Jesus is coming into existence in Latin America.[5] A new spirituality is in the germinal stage there; because it is germinal it cannot as yet be sketched out in detail for the purposes of labeling it and circumscribing it by characteristic traits. At present we are in the position of those trying to decide whom a newborn child resembles. Some will say the father, others the mother; some will even find that the child has this grandfather's nose or that aunt's eyes, whereas still others will even be of the opinion that the child does not remind them of any family features known to them. Better to photograph the child and decide later on whom it resembles.

I am aware of this difficulty. But lest I dwell too long on the point, I shall take the risk of singling out some characteristic features of the spirituality that is now developing in Latin America. What I shall really be attempting is to organize certain experiences and the reflections they provoke; we still lack the necessary perspective and distance to proceed in any other fashion. The traits I shall point out will therefore not be sharply defined and will call for a good deal of nuancing; some of them may have to be dropped, others added.

As in the case of other spiritual ways that I have previously called to the reader's attention, the major themes of collective Christian experience in Latin America are those proper to Christian existence in its entirety. Here, too, reorganization is being carried out in view of some central intuitions regarding the demands of the historical moment. Our experiences in the framework of commitment to the poor and oppressed of Latin America are sending us back to fundamental ideas in the gospels. It could not be otherwise. These experiences are suggesting new approaches and raising new questions.[6] But at the same time the biblical message is challenging our experiences and shedding light on them.

I shall keep this circular relationship in mind when trying to suggest some features of the spirituality that is arising among us. The experience of solidarity calls for a conversion, which is the point of departure for any following of Jesus. A commitment within history calls for effective action within history, but the effort to achieve efficacy brings with it a deeper penetration into God's gratuitous love as the source of everything else and as a power that sweeps us along with it. The Latin American situation is characterized by profound suffering out of which comes a new, paschal experience of joy that flows from the gift of life. "Inhuman" and "anti-evangelical" poverty is a massive reality in our midst, but commitment to the poor and the oppressed leads to the rediscovery of a central gospel theme: spiritual childhood. Solidarity with the dispossessed has brought many Christians a painful experience of loneliness due to the isolation into which they are thrown, the suspicion that their actions arouse, or the imprisonment they suffer; this loneliness proves nonetheless to be a privileged means of grasping the deeper meaning of ecclesial community.

I think that the characteristic traits of the "walking according to the Lord'' that is developing in Latin America are due to the relationships I have just described. It is important, however, not to isolate the various factors, because only when they are interconnected is it possible to grasp what is peculiar to each of the traits. When they are linked as I have linked them we shall perhaps better understand what it means to live in community or what the attitude of spiritual childhood really is. Joy in the gratuitous gift of God's love calls upon us to break with sin, injustice, and death in contemporary Latin America.

As I attempt to sketch a profile of the new way that is coming into existence among us, I shall illustrate what I am saying by stringing together texts that attempt to express the spiritual experiences that are at the heart of solidarity with the poor and dispossessed. I make no claim to completeness. The subject deserves a more comprehensive and detailed book that is presently beyond my abilities. The texts I shall cite are meant to be representative of many others, perhaps even others that are far richer. My purpose here is simply a first approach to the subject.

The fact is that daily contact with the experiences of some, a reading of the writings of many, and the testimony of still others have convinced me of the profound spiritual experiences that persons among us are having today. They are a gift from the Lord and therefore have a good deal of the ineffable about them. My hope is that what I say will not betray, even if it inevitably diminishes, the way in which the presence of the God of life is being experienced in these lands of premature and unjustly inflicted death.

6

CONVERSION:
A REQUIREMENT FOR SOLIDARITY

A conversion is the starting point of every spiritual journey.[1] It involves a break with the life lived up to that point; it is a prerequisite for entering the kingdom: "The time is fulfilled, and the kingdom of God is at hand; repent, and believe in the gospel" (Mark 1:15). It presupposes also, and above all, that one decides to set out on a new path: "Sell all that you have . . . and come, follow me" (Luke 18:22).[2] Without this second aspect the break would lack the focus that a fixed horizon provides and would ultimately be deprived of meaning.

Because of this second aspect a conversion is not something that is done once and for all. It entails a development, even a painful one, that is not without uncertainties, doubts, and temptations to turn back on the road that has been traveled. The experience of the Jewish people after its departure from Egypt is still prototypical here. Fidelity to the word of God implies a permanent conversion. This is a central theme in the teaching of the prophets.

On the other hand, the path of conversion is not one marked only by stumbling blocks; there is a growth in maturity. Throughout the gospels we are repeatedly told that after some word or deed of Jesus "his disciples believed in him." The point of this statement is not that up to that point they had no faith, but rather that their faith deepened with the passage of time. To believe in

God is more than simply to profess God's existence; it is to enter into communion with God and—the two being inseparable—with our fellow human beings as well. And all this adds up to a process.

Break and Solidarity

Break, new way, steps forward and backward—this entire movement is subject to the call and action of the Spirit who requires of us a decision that leads us to think, feel, and live with Christ in our day-to-day lives (Phil. 2:5). This requirement is seen as especially urgent by Christians committed, in one way or another, to the liberation of the poor in Latin America.

The upshot of the option for the poor and their liberation is that in contemporary Latin America we are in a period characterized by a great effort at solidarity. Solidarity is seen as a concrete expression of Christian love today, which seeks roots in the cultural traditions of the indigenous peoples of Latin America. A hasty and simplistic interpretation of the liberationist perspective has led some to affirm that its dominant, if not exclusive, themes are commitment, the social dimension of faith, the denunciation of injustices, and others of a similar nature. It is said that the liberationist impulse leaves little room for grasping the necessity of personal conversion as a condition for Christian life and for being aware of the place that sin and repentance have in our lives.

Such an interpretation and criticism are simply caricatures. One need only have contact with the Christians in question to appreciate the complexity of their approach and the depth of their spiritual experience. In the movement of solidarity with the poor and exploited there is no attempt to downplay the importance of the breaks that the gospel demands of us as a requirement for accepting the message of the kingdom; if anything, the movement calls rather for an emphasis on this factor. The period of solidarity that men and women are experiencing in Latin America is leading to a new grasp of the importance of conversion; in doing so it gives us insight into aspects of which no account is taken in other approaches, and it is perhaps this that is confusing some observers.

Acknowledgment of Sin

In our relationship with God and with others there is an inescapable personal dimension: to reject a fellow human—a possibility implicit in our freedom—is to reject God as well. Conversion implies that we recognize the presence of sin in our lives and our world. In other words, we see and admit what is vitiating our relationship with God and our solidarity with others— what, in consequence, is also hindering the creation of a just and human society. The situation of tragic poverty in which Latin America is living only intensifies this awareness on our part.

To sin is to deny love, to resist welcoming the kingdom of God. Many of those who are committed to the poor freely admit the difficulties they have, as human beings and believers, in loving God and neighbor and therefore their need of repentance and a break with deviant practices. A Christian community in Lima writes: "There are defects in our lives. Sin is among us too, and we are not always faithful. We do not always live up to our commitments; there are little betrayals, acts of cowardice, falls, selfish and underhanded actions." Unless we see our personal connivances with elements that are keeping an inhuman and unjust situation in existence, we run the risk of pharisaism: of seeing the speck in our neighbor's eye but not the beam in our own.

One type of connivance, which is clearer today now that we have a better knowledge of our social reality, takes the form of sins of omission: "We regard ourselves as guilty for keeping silence in the face of the events agitating our country. In the face of repression, detentions, the economic crisis, the loss of jobs by so many workers, murders and tortures, we have kept silent as though we did not belong to that world."[3] The cowardice that keeps silent in the face of the sufferings of the poor and that offers any number of adroit justifications represents an especially serious failure of Latin American Christians. However, it is not always easy to be lucid in this regard.

In addition, the bishops at Medellín, after speaking of individual failures, went on to say: "When speaking of injustice, we refer to those realities that constitute a sinful situation"

("Peace," no. 1). Despite the reactions to this point in some circles, Puebla endorsed what Medellín had said[4] and followed closely the guidelines set down by John Paul II in his Mexican addresses that were delivered during the very days when the episcopal conference was being held.[5]

Insofar, then, as a conversion is a break with sin it will have to have both a personal and a social dimension. The Episcopal Conference of Peru has stated:

> The good news we proclaim is not simply a past event; it has to do with the needs and aspirations of the human beings who hear it. At the same time it is an energetic call to a conversion that, although affecting the deepest recesses of the human person, is not limited to interior life but must also be translated into attitudes and commitments that regard changes in reality as a requirement of Christian love.[6]

Cardinal Juan Landázuri, archbishop of Lima, repeated the same urgent call: "At the present time our native land is undergoing a painful crisis in which the high social cost paid in hunger and undernourishment, sickness, and death, lack of education and jobs . . . falls with special cruelty on the vast majority of our people. At such a time the call for personal conversion and social change becomes particularly ugent."[7]

The change called for is not simply an interior one but one that involves the entire person as a corporeal being (a factor of human solidarity, as we saw when considering Pauline texts, above) and therefore also has consequences for the web of social relationships of which the individual is a part. That is why Archbishop Romero could make this strong statement: "Nowadays an authentic Christian conversion must lead to an unmasking of the social mechanisms that turn the worker and the peasant into marginalized persons. Why do the rural poor become part of society only in the coffee-and cotton-picking seasons?"[8] The will to conversion should lead to this kind of concrete analysis.

For a long time this perspective has perhaps been absent from the treatment of the theme in spiritual literature; today, however, it cannot be neglected.[9] The encounter with the Lord in the inmost recesses of the individual does not exclude but rather calls for a similar encounter in the depths of the wretchedness in which the poor of our countries live. In these poor, Puebla tells us, "we ought to recognize the suffering features of Christ the Lord, who questions and challenges us" (no. 31). But how can we do this and achieve solidarity with the poor if we do not understand the structural causes of "this situation of pervasive extreme poverty" (ibid.) that gives rise to the suffering?

The consequences of such a recognition are clear. It becomes necessary for us to examine our own responsibility for the existence of unjust "social mechanisms." In addition to calling for a personal transformation, the analysis will in many cases mean a break with the social milieu to which we belong. The conversion required will have to be radical enough to bring us into a different world, the world of the poor. I shall return to this point.

As we saw above from our study of passages in St. Paul, sin means death. This is true both of personal sin and of the situation of sin in which Latin America is living. A commitment to the poor makes us see this truth with a new urgency, as Archbishop Romero put it:

> Now we realize what sin is. We realize that offenses against God bring death to human beings. We realize that sin is truly death-dealing; not only does it bring the interior death of the one who commits it; it also produces real, objective death. We are thus reminded of a basic truth of our Christian faith. Sin caused the death of the Son of God; sin continues to cause the death of the children of God.[10]

This is a clear and profound statement that raises questions and points to new paths.

The Way of Life

To acknowledge one's sins implies the will to restore broken amity, to which we are called by petition for pardon and reconciliation. The God of the Bible manifests fidelity and mercy in a permanent disposition to pardon: "The steadfast love of the Lord never ceases, his mercies never come to an end" (Lam. 3: 22–23).

This attitude of God must serve as a model for the people of God. As Micah puts it, "He has showed you, O man, what is good; and what does the Lord require of you but to do justice, and to love kindness, and to walk humbly with your God?" (6:8). Pardon is an inherent characteristic of the Christian community. To pardon means not to fixate the past, but to create possibilities for persons to change and to realign the course of their lives. The Lord does not want us to have an "evil eye," trying to ossify persons and situations in movement; the Lord is good, merciful, and open to what is new (Matt. 20:15). Pardon forges community.

The Bible tells us of a God who is faithful to and mindful of the divine deeds of the past, but also ready to forget, out of love, the failings of a sinful people. The psalmist can exclaim: "Thou didst withdraw all thy wrath; thou didst turn from thy hot anger" (85:3–4). Pardon implies forgetting, canceling out a past of death and initiating a new era characterized by life. The psalmist would have us say confidently to the Lord: "Wilt thou not revive us again, that thy people may rejoice in thee?" (85:6).

The Lord is the one to whom we say, "Thou dost show me the path of life" (16:11). Exactly so!

The new way that conversion and pardon opens up takes the form of an option in behalf of life. The option finds expression particularly in solidarity with those who are subject to "a premature and unjust death." The bishop and priests of Machala, Ecuador, have stated:

As the followers of Christ that we are trying to be, we cannot fail to show our solidarity with the suffering—the imprisoned, the marginalized, the persecuted—for Christ identifies himself with them (Matt. 25:31–46). We once again assure the people of our support and our service in the fulfillment of our specific mission as preachers of the gospel of Jesus Christ who came to proclaim the good news to the poor and freedom to the oppressed (Luke 4:18).[11]

This solidarity is not only with isolated individuals. To be poor is something much vaster and more complete than simply belonging to a specific social group (social class, culture, ethnos). By the same token, the context of a collectivity whose destiny is shared, willy-nilly, by the great majority of a given population must be taken into account. If, then, in our activity we try to separate them from their own world, we are not really in solidarity with them. If we love others, we love them in their social context. This requirement makes commitment more demanding but also more authentic.

For analogous reasons this way of solidarity is not to be undertaken by isolated individuals. It should be done along with the entire church. "We affirm," said the bishops at Puebla, "the need for conversion on the part of the whole church to a preferential option for the poor, an option aimed at their integral liberation" (PD, no. 1134; cf. 1157, 1158). This conversion entails a break with a previous situation in which for one or another reason solidarity with the poor either did not exist or existed only as a possibility. This represents a deep-seated conviction among Latin American Christians, and bishops laid a special emphasis on it even before Puebla. The Episcopal Conference of Guatemala has said: "The entire church of Guatemala must take part in the process of conversion in order that it may be an efficacious sign of Christ's presence in society and a suitable instrument in God's hands for contributing to the building of a better homeland."[12]

Conversion is a requirement for the solidarity that is part of the task of the church. Clergymen in Santiago, Chile, have stated:

> The bishops are conscious that one element in the mission of the church is to take up the work of solidarity, because in the final analysis solidarity is just another name for the ancient commandment the church has received from Jesus Christ. It used to be called mercy, then charity, then commitment; today it is called solidarity. To give food to the hungry . . . drink to the thirsty . . . clothing to the naked . . . shelter to the homeless . . . and to welcome the stranger are actions so basic that at the end of time we shall have to render an account of them. Solidarity is written into the very substance of the church, and

therefore there can be no drawing back from the work needed to achieve it.[13]

In point of fact, the various terms mentioned are not perfectly interchangeable. They express different aspects of a single ecclesial function that the term "solidarity" serves to define very accurately in our day, for, as John Paul II has said, solidarity is a proof of the fidelity of the church to its Lord.[14]

The Material and the Spiritual

In the context of solidarity with the poor and oppressed, that which is often referred to as "the material" takes on a meaning it does not seem to have had before. The aspects of Pauline theology that we studied above, in part 2, will be a great help here in gaining a better understanding of this point.

In recent decades an important revolution, and one ratified by Vatican II, has taken place in Christian experience and thought with regard to the value set on earthly realities.[15] This has led, among other results, to a new approach to the human body, despite reservations on the part of some. Encouraged by this new perspective, some Christian milieus, usually in affluent countries, have promoted a reevaluation and "celebration" of the human body in cultural expressions—for example, some modern dances and other bodily forms of expression that are used in eucharistic celebrations. In their desire to break with a spirituality that they think belittles or neglects the physical side of their lives, these Christians emphasize the importance of the bodily expressions of Christian life; more broadly, they stress the rights of the body (their own bodies) in human life.

Whatever be the merits of this claim, I want to note here that the concern for the corporeal in contemporary Latin American spiritual experiences has come about in quite a different way. There is no question here of a preoccupation with the physical and material dimensions of our individual selves. In our world, there has been a breakthrough of the material because the vast majorities are in urgent need of bread, medicine, housing, and so on. The physical in question is located at the level of the basic necessities of the human person. It is not "*my* body" but the "body of

the poor person''—the weak and languishing body of the poor—
that has made the material a part of a spiritual outlook.[16] The goal
is to liberate that body from the forces of death, and this liberation entails a walking according to the Spirit who is life. In this,
Paul is a guide without equal.

The religious aspirations of the poor do not eliminate their
physical hunger, and we must keep both of these dimensions before us. As Rutilio Grande recalled, ''It was correctly said during
our Archdiocesan Pastoral Week that 'our people are hungry for
the true God and they are hungry for bread.' And no privileged
minority has any right, from the Christian standpoint, to exist in
isolation in our country; it can exist only in function of the great
majorities that make up the Salvadoran people.''[17] The concrete
conditions in which the poor live help us to grasp the scope of our
own conversion to the Lord. As Bishop Leonidas Proaño has put
it:

> If conversion should be a turning to God and neighbor . . .
> then we must ask ourselves whether we perhaps do not show
> greater respect to images made of wood than to human beings
> who are the living images of God. We must ask ourselves
> whether we are not more courteous to images than to the hu-
> man beings who are sunk in ignorance, sorrow, poverty, and
> slavery.[18]

A concern for the material needs of the poor is an element in
our spirituality.[19] The sincerity of our conversion to the Lord is to
be judged by the action to which this concern leads us. A joint
statement of grassroots communities in Managua, Nicaragua,
reads in part:

> We committed Christians who sign this document are trying to
> strip ourselves of the old person and embody in ourselves the
> new person by following Christ our brother. He rejects (Mark
> 2:21–22) a spirituality that is nothing but an idealist frame of
> mind and accepts only one that leads to a commitment to
> clothing the naked, educating the ignorant, and so on. Today
> more than ever before the words of Christ have special mean-
> ing: what you do to the most wretched you do to me.[20]

There is an echo here, once again, of Matthew 25:31–46. The concrete and definitional character of this passage has long made it play an outstanding role in the spiritual experience of Latin American Christians.[21] The text cannot be properly interpreted except by situating it within the gospel message as a whole. I shall look at other aspects of it further on; for the moment let me emphasize only one of its main thrusts.

The text is one of the many in the gospels that underscore the importance of action in behalf of the poor in the following of Jesus. I made this point above, in part 2, when I spoke of our encounter with the Lord. But there is something distinctive in the passage from Matthew: it reminds us that what we do to the poor we do to Christ himself. It is this fact that gives action in behalf of the poor its decisive character and prevents it from being taken simply as an expression of the "social dimension" of faith. No, it is much more than that; such action has an element of contemplation, of encounter with God, at the very heart of the work of love. And this encounter is not "merited" by any work; it is the gratuitous gift of the Lord. This is what the passage in question makes known to us, and in so doing it evokes our surprise ("When did we see you hungry?").

This is a work of love that implies a gift of self and is not simply a matter of fulfilling a duty. It is a work of concrete, authentic love for the poor that is not possible apart from a certain integration into their world and apart from bonds of real friendship with those who suffer despoliation and injustice.[22] The solidarity is not with "the poor" in the abstract but with human beings of flesh and bone. Without love and affection, without—why not say it?—tenderness, there can be no true gesture of solidarity. Where these are lacking there is an impersonality and coldness (however well intentioned and accompanied by a desire for justice) that the flesh-and-blood poor will not fail to perceive. True love exists only among equals, "for love effects a likeness between the lover and the object loved."[23] And this supposes an ability to approach others and respect their sensitivities.[24]

Consistency and Stubbornness

The new way that we undertake and to which we are constantly being converted calls for constancy and deep conviction: "At present we are a people that knows only pain. We endure in darkness, with the stubborn certainty that some day a pure and free human being and human society will be born."[25]

The stubbornness we often find in the great saints is nothing but the expression of a profound fidelity that does not bow to difficulties and obstacles. A great Chilean bishop, recently deceased, said: "We believe that our identity as Christians and as a church is being purified and deepened by every conflict, provided that we try first and foremost to be faithful to the Spirit of Jesus Christ who is guiding the one history of salvation and integral liberation for the poor and for all humankind."[26]

Spirituality as an all-embracing attitude is precisely a force that bestows constancy and prevents our being "tossed to and fro and carried about with every wind of doctrine" (Eph. 4:14). This stubbornness—for that is what I am talking about—has its source in hope, "for we know," as a statement by Guatemalan religious formulates it, "that after the 'torments of unleashed violence' that now afflict us, the sun of justice of God our Father will shine again. We will not betray our cause even though it brings us persecution and death, because we trust that Christ is present in the tragic reality that is our present life."[27]

Hope often finds support in the testimonies of those who have been called to give up their lives. Archbishop Romero, in one of his homilies, said:

> Lord, this day our conversion and faith draw support from those who lie there in their coffins. They are messengers who convey the reality of our people and the noble aspirations of a church that seeks naught but the salvation of the people. See, Lord, the multitude that is gathered in your cathedral is itself the prayer of a people that groans and weeps but does not despair, because it knows that Christ did not lie: the kingdom is indeed at hand and requires only that we be converted and believe in it.[28]

This is the prayer of a pastor and brother who sustains the hope of his people.

In the gospels fear and inconstancy are seen as failures of faith. Jesus' exhortation to his disciples, "Have no fear" (e.g., Matt. 14:27), has a positive meaning: have faith, know how to trust.

Paul frequently calls upon his communities to "be steadfast in faith." An authentic and solid spirituality will prevent our being easily shaken in our commitments and our Christian life. Teresa of Avila says of those who would have such steadfastness:

> It is most important—all-important, indeed—that they should begin well by making an earnest and most determined resolve not to halt . . . whatever may come, whatever may happen to them, however hard they may have to labor, whoever may complain of them, whether they reach their goal or die on the road . . . whether the very world dissolves before them.[29]

This "determined resolve" is what I have been calling "stubbornness." It is the steadfastness of those who are convinced, those who know what they want, those who put their trust in the Lord and devote their lives to others: "Those who trust in the Lord are like Mount Zion, which cannot be moved, but abides forever" (Ps. 125:1).

The solidarity required by the preferential option for the poor forces us back to a fundamental Christian attitude: a grasp of the need for continual conversion. We are then able to find in the break with former ways and in our chosen new way deeper dimensions of a personal and social, material and spiritual, kind. The conversion to the Lord to which solidarity with the oppressed brings us calls for stubbornness and constancy on the road we have undertaken.

7

GRATUITOUSNESS:
THE ATMOSPHERE FOR EFFICACY

Entry into a historical process is generally accompanied by a desire that one's participation in it may be realistic and effective. This concern is an inescapable element in the life experience of Latin American Christians. For it is not possible to struggle against injustice and yet not analyze the causes of the injustice and the possible ways of dealing with them. Statements that never go beyond principles are naive and in the long run lead to self-deception; they are a way of evading history—the place where our fidelity to the Lord must find expression at the present time.

On the other hand, biblical testimony is clear that the encounter with God results from divine initiative that creates an impact of gratitude, which should permeate the entire Christian life. How do we live these two dimensions?

Efficacious Love

In the face of a manner of Christian life that gave subjective intentions a privileged rank and was unconcerned about objective results, the necessity of making love an effective force within history is forcing men and women to find other spiritual ways. They are truly searching, not simply abandoning spiritual perspectives, as some, afraid that old ways may disappear, sometimes seem to think.

This concern was already present, though in a different context of course, in Ignatian spirituality. Ignatius's emphasis on effective action and on a prudent charity has often been misunderstood and even made the subject of biting commentary. It seems to me, however, that it represents an important contribution to Christian spirituality, and this at the threshold of the modern age, at a time when the human race was acquiring a new grasp of its own historical reality and of the possibilities of changing this reality. It was an awareness that has been sharpened with the passage of time, bringing with it important demands for the following of Jesus today.

Authentic love tries to start with the concrete needs of the other and not with the "duty" of practicing love. Love is respectful of others and therefore feels obliged to base its action on an analysis of their situation and needs. Works in behalf of the neighbor are not done in order to channel idle energies or to give available personnel something to do; they are done because the other has needs and it is urgent that we attend to them. In Latin America today, many of these needs are found at the most elementary levels of physical survival.

It is important to note that, contrary to what some may think, this desire for effectiveness gives a new force to the experience of gratuitousness. This experience is not meant to serve as a refuge for historical powerlessness (which is to be rejected as an unchristian attitude), but rather sets up a demand for real and effective commitment. As Archbishop Romero acutely remarked: "The world of the poor teaches us the form Christian love must take . . . that it must indeed be gratuitous but that it must also seek to be effective in history."[1]

Concern for effective action is a way of expressing love for the other. The gratuitousness of the gift of the kingdom does not do away with effective action but rather calls for it all the more. "In the presence of this God who acts gratuitously we must show society a reign that is not reducible to energy expended in the service of human development, but that has its source in an encounter with a personal God with whom intimacy is bestowed as a *gift* and who, once given to us, neither suppresses nor competes with the human *effort* to build a better world."[2]

It would be easy to conclude, especially in this age of "antidualism," that what is required of us is a synthesis of gratuitousness and effectiveness. There is something to this, but at the same time the subject is a more complex one and calls for greater discernment. A well-known text from the Ignatian spiritual tradition may offer a fruitful approach: "In matters which he [Ignatius] took up pertaining to the service of our Lord, he made use of all the human means to succeed in them, with a care and efficiency as great as if the success depended on these means; and he confided in God and depended on his providence as greatly as if all the other human means which he was using were of no effect."[3]

What we have here is more than a synthesis. Gratuitousness is an atmosphere in which the entire quest for effectiveness is bathed. It is something both subtler and richer than a balance maintained between two important aspects. This alternative perspective does not represent an abandonment of efficacy but rather seeks to locate efficacy in a comprehensive and fully human context that is in accord with the gospel. That context is the space of freely bestowed encounter with the Lord. A gratuitous encounter is mysterious and it draws us into itself. Many Latin American Christians are attempting to live the gratuitous love of God by committing themselves to a liberative undertaking.

A matter of great importance to the faith arises at this point. Paul, requesting that others in the community (*koinonia*) collaborate "for the poor among the saints at Jerusalem" (Rom. 15:26), a task on which he lays great emphasis,[4] writes with tact and clarity: "I say this not as a command, but to prove by the earnestness of others that your love also is genuine" (2 Cor. 8:8). There is nothing more urgent than gratitude, for it "proves" that love is "genuine."

Everything Is Grace

The experience and idea of the gratuitousness of God's love are fundamental and of central importance in the Christian life.[5] The gratuitous initiative of the Lord is a dominant theme in Pauline theology ("The free gift in the grace of that one man Jesus Christ abounded for many" [Rom. 5:15]), as also later in Augustinian theology.

"God first loved us" (1 John 4:19). Everything starts from there. The gift of God's love is the source of our being and puts its impress on our lives. We have been made by love and for love. Only by loving, then, can we fulfill ourselves as persons; that is how we respond to the initiative taken by God's love.[6]

God's love for us is gratuitous; we do not merit it. It is a gift we receive before we exist, or, to be more accurate, a gift in view of which we have been created. Election to adoptive filiation comes first:

> Blessed be the God and Father of our Lord Jesus Christ, who has blessed us in Christ with every spiritual blessing in the heavenly places, even as he chose us in him before the foundation of the world, that we should be holy and blameless before him. He destined us in love to be his sons through Jesus Christ, according to the purpose of his will [Eph. 1:3–5].

Gratuitousness thus marks our lives so that we are led to love gratuitously and to want to be loved gratuitously. It is a profoundly human characteristic. Such is our makeup. True love is always a gift, something that transcends motives and merits. As is said so beautifully in the Canticle of Canticles, "Many waters cannot quench love, neither can floods drown it. If a man offered for love all the wealth of his house, it would be utterly scorned" (8:7). Gratitude is the space of that radical self-giving and that presence of beauty in our lives without which even the struggle for justice would be crippled.[7]

If this is true of human life as a whole, it is particularly true in the matter that concerns us here. The experience of gratuitousness is the space of encounter with the Lord. Unless we understand the meaning of gratuitousness, there will be no contemplative dimension in our life. Contemplation is not a state of paralysis but of radical self-giving, as we saw in reading passages from John of the Cross. In the final analysis, to believe in God means to live our life as a gift from God and to look upon everything that happens in it as a manifestation of this gift.

In saying all this I am not trying to ignore the coherence proper to history (the realm of what Thomistic theology calls "second causes"). On the contrary, my intention is to penetrate to the deepest meaning of history and, in the words of Ignatius of Loyola, to "find God in all things." But the fact is that the attitude of finding God in all things can be acquired only if we can activate a contemplative dimension in our lives. Contemplation disposes us to recognize that "everything is grace," to use an expression of Bernanos, which in fact comes from Thérèse of Lisieux, who, contrary to the deformed image of her that has long been passed on to us, was indeed a powerful saint.

Prayer is an expression of faith and trust in the Lord; it is an act that is peculiar to and characteristic of the believer. It takes place in the context of the love that we know to be marked in its very source by gratuitousness. Prayer is in fact a loving dialogue, to use the description given by Teresa of Avila.[8] It arises as a humble and trusting response to the Father's gratuitous gift of love and expresses our desire to share that gift in an unaffected way with our brothers and sisters. Mary's canticle says it well: "My soul magnifies the Lord, and my spirit rejoices in God my Savior, for he has regarded the low estate of his handmaiden" (Luke 1: 46–48).

Like every dialogue of love, prayer runs the risk of being interpreted as a "useless activity," whereas in point of fact it is precisely an experience of a gratuitousness that creates new forms of communication. It is expressed, for example, in the silence proper to prayer, as indeed to every loving encounter (human experience bears witness to this). A moment comes when words can no longer communicate the depth of what is experienced. Simple and silent presence is a touchstone of love.

From gratuitousness also comes the language of symbols. The experience of human love leads us to recognize that "rites are necessary," as Antoine de Saint-Exupéry said. We resort to symbols in the liturgy, in community prayer: they move within the ambit of the language of gratuitous love.

I said in part 1 that some sectors of the Latin American church are passing through a time of prayer.[9] It is surprising to see a people becoming increasingly better organized and more effective in the struggle to assert its rights to life and justice[10] and at the same time giving evidence of a profound sense of prayer and of a conviction that in the final analysis love and peace are an unmerited gift of God.[11]

In their religious celebrations, whether at especially important moments or in the circumstances of everyday life, the poor turn to the Lord with the trustfulness and spontaneity of a child who speaks to its father and tells him of its suffering and hopes.[12] One Christian community that had suffered a harsh trial writes with simplicity: "We tell all our Christian brothers and sisters that we have the courage to continue to celebrate our faith in groups as often as we can."[13] "As often as we can": the harsh situation in which a people lives forces it to pray "in the catacombs."

A Twofold Movement

Earlier I pointed out the important part that Matthew 25:31–46 plays in the Latin American spiritual experience. The passage is a great help in grasping the requirement of effective action in the service of the other. And indeed not only of effective action but also of what we might call the "earthiness" of Christian love, in contrast to a spiritualistic interpretation of that love. The Matthean text makes it easier to understand that encounter with the poor through concrete works is a necessary step in view of encounter with Christ himself.

But we have also come to understand that a true and full encounter with our neighbor requires that we first experience the gratuitousness of God's love. Once we have experienced it, our approach to others is purified of any tendency to impose an alien will on them; it is disinterested and respectful of their personalities, their needs and aspirations. The other is our way for reaching God, but our relationship with God is a precondition for encounter and true communion with the other. It is not possible to separate these two movements, which are perhaps really only a single movement: Jesus Christ, who is God and man, is our way to the Father but he is also our way to recognition of others as brothers and sisters.[14] The experience of the gratuitousness of God's love— which is a basic datum of the Christian faith—is not simply a kind of historical parenthesis as it were; rather it gives human becoming its full meaning. A realization of this is gradually becoming a basic element in the spiritual experience now coming into existence in Latin America.

I am aware of the limitations of what I have been saying. The experience is not universal, nor is it always explicit, nor, on the other hand, is it entirely new. Moreover, an inevitable inertia is still with us. Nonetheless a significant dynamism is clearly forming. The experience of gratuitousness is not a form of evasion but rather the locus of life and the reality that envelops and permeates the endeavor to achieve historical efficacy. This efficacy will be sought with ever increasing fervor in the measure that it reveals to us the gratuitous love of God: God's preference for the poor.

A commitment that takes shape in effective action is therefore required by the gratuitous love of the Lord, but let us not forget that an inverse moment is also needed: the contemplation that historical action calls for.[15]

8

JOY: VICTORY OVER SUFFERING

If we trace the deeper currents at work in what is happening in Latin America, we find that they always lead us into worlds of hope and joy. This must not make us forget, of course, the great suffering caused today by entrenched death-dealing conditions, or the further suffering inflicted by the sophisticated and cruel repression that those (inside and outside Latin America) who refuse to surrender their privileges have introduced.

All those who are trying to live in close proximity to the poor will bear witness to the intermeshing afflictions that form a chain and turn the life of the poor into a prison existence. Despite the fact that the vast majority of these sufferings are caused by a situation that is inhuman and unjust, and should therefore in principle be changed, yet so closely are these sufferings bound up with the entire social order, and so all-encompassing and resistant to change is this order itself, that many feel helpless and discouraged with regard to any concrete possibility of altering it.

It is a frightening and deeply saddening experience to come in contact, through conversations and through pastoral work among the people, with the miseries that descend upon the poor in an endless procession. There are countless small things: wants of every kind, the abuse and contempt that the poor endure, lives tormented by the search for employment, incredible ways of earning a living or—more accurately—earning a crust of bread, mean bickerings, separations of family members, sicknesses not found at other levels of society, infant undernourishment and death, unjust prices for products and commodities, total confusion about what is necessary for themselves and their families, delinquency springing from abandonment or despair, the loss of one's own cultural values.

Small things, perhaps, when taken in isolation and looked at in the abstract, but as human sufferings they take on vast dimensions and force us to recoil in horror. If to all this we add the repression that is worsening in Latin America and is on its way to becoming part of daily life, then we have a picture of suffering and death. Worst of all: the suffering and death are inflicted by the unjust hand and the greedy heart.

But those who have the painful experience I have been describing also know that something new is germinating in this universe of unmerited afflictions: the self-consciousness of a people now expressing itself in organizations and in its experience of a liberating faith. The result is that many are giving their lives in a struggle against death. Therefore, too, the element of hope that this people is beginning to experience, which brings it joy. The opposite of joy is not suffering, but sadness, as was said during a workshop on popular spirituality in Peru. This joy is not easily attained but it is real. It is not the superficial kind of rejoicing that springs from unawareness or resignation, but the joy born of the conviction that unjust mistreatment and suffering will be overcome.[1] This is a paschal joy proper to a time of martyrdom.

The believing poor have never lost their capacity for having a good time and celebrating, despite the harsh conditions in which they live: today this capacity is being expanded by hope. The result of this for the Christian groups most committed to the suffering and oppressed poor is a deeper understanding of what it means to live the Easter message.

Schooling in Martyrdom

In contemporary Latin America, supporting the defense of the right of the poor to life easily leads to suffering and even death.[2] This outcome, which is only seemingly paradoxical, reveals the depth of the resistance that must be overcome in changing the implanted situation of "anti-evangelical poverty."

Cardinal Landázuri writes:

To carry the cross is not simply to endure the inevitable hardships of life; it is also, and in present circumstances must be, to accept the sufferings imposed by the struggle against injustice and oppression. It means to suffer in the attempt to change what Medellín called "a sinful situation" ("Peace," no. 16) that has evidently crystalized in the unjust structures that are characteristic of Latin America (cf. "Justice," no. 1).[3]

This describes the situation very accurately. It is a situation that today is producing many hardships: suspicion, calumny, systematic attacks, imprisonment, torture, exile, persecution of the church.[4] Yet all this is also leading to a purification and strengthening of commitment.

The gift of self can go as far as physical death. It has rightly been said that every spirituality has martyrdom as one of its dimensions. Martyrdom is certainly a dominant note in the spiritual experience many among us are having today. The Guatemalan bishops write:

Faith makes us realize that the church in Guatemala is passing through a time of grace and positive hope. Persecution has always been an obvious sign of fidelity to Christ and his gospel. The blood of our martyrs will be the seed of many new Christians, and it is a consolation for us to see that we are enduring our share of the sufferings still lacking in the passion of Christ (Col. 1:24) for the redemption of the world.[5]

In speaking of martyrs I am obviously not making any formal proclamation on the point; that falls within the competency of others in the church. I am trying only to express the value we set on the witness (Greek: *martyria*) of those who give their lives because they believe in the God of life and because they love the dispossessed.[6] The blood of these victims marks a fruitful path for us to follow as Christians. "Let us remain in communion with the martyrs. They are laying the strongest foundations for that divine city that is rising up toward eternity."[7]

Amid all our admiration and respect for martyrdom we must not forget the cruelty that marks such an event, the abhorrence that the conditions giving rise to these murders should make us feel. Martyrdom is something that happens but is not sought.[8] This statement of Luis Espinal seems to me profoundly sound and Christian:

> The faithful do not have a vocation to be martyrs. When they fall in the struggle, they fall with simplicity and without posing. . . . Life ought to be given by working, not by dying. Away with the slogans that create a cult of death! . . . The revolution calls for human beings who are lucidly conscious; realists who have ideals. And if the day comes when they must give their lives, they will do it with the simplicity of someone who is carrying out one more task, without melodramatic gestures.[9]

This passage becomes all the more striking when we recall that Espinal was murdered shortly after writing it. His is not an isolated outlook. After the bishop and pastoral ministers of El Quiché were forced to withdraw from the area under threat of death, the Christian communities there wrote:

> On Christmas, New Year's, and other feast days some priests have been coming here and celebrating Mass in several villages. This gives us a great deal of joy, but at the same time we are grieved because the priests may be killed. We want them to come, we want Bishop Girardi and the fathers and sisters to come, *but not now*. We want them to stay alive and take care of themselves so that they can go on helping the people, now and later, as they have always done.[10]

Let them come, "but not now," for they want them to stay alive. It is precisely the affirmation of life that brings full appreciation of the meaning of martyrdom. The simple statement of the communities of El Quiché reminds us of this truth.

Easter Joy

The daily suffering of the poor and the surrender of their lives in the struggle against the causes of their situation have given new power to the Easter message. The deaths of so many in Latin

America, whether anonymous individuals or persons better known, have made possible a deeper understanding of the Lord's resurrection. Joy springs therefore from the hope that death is not the final word of history. As Hugo Echegaray writes: "In the restrictive situations in which the poor find themselves forced to live, they repeatedly encounter the cross of Jesus, which resulted from his option for fellowship. They thereby enter into the experience of the resurrection, which is life in the midst of the death that the system scatters as it goes."[11]

When Fr. João-Bosco Burnier was murdered at a police station where he had gone to protest the mistreatment of two women, Bishop Pedro Casaldáliga, who went with him, wrote:

> He died for justice and charity. In Amazonia. At an especially critical time, a time of martyrs. . . . Pray that we may be faithful, that the Spirit will keep giving us the gift of joy, that the church may bear witness to the very end. . . . The Lord is the resurrection and the life. And the communion of the entire church is with us. And this death and these threats serve as a witness to others, "outside," who are also struggling for the new humankind. This is not a sad time, but a beautiful gospel time.[12]

"A beautiful gospel time," filled with a resurrection joy that is only rendered more intense when some bear witness to their commitment even to the point of death.[13]

Hope of the resurrection is in no sense an evasion of concrete history; on the contrary, it leads to a redoubling of effort in the struggle against what brings unjust death. "The resurrection of the Lord prevents his messengers from being reduced to being the outriders of an inhuman system, allayers of conflict, servants of the powerful, anesthetists of so-called primitive or savage peoples so that deadly cultural transplants may be carried out."[14] Belief in the resurrection is incompatible with the acceptance of a society that condemns the poor to death. To be aware of this, and to act accordingly, is a central aspect of being "witnesses to Easter."[15]

This testimony will not be given without a struggle against a combination of bitterness and discouragement, for these two temptations are inevitable given the enormous resistance that must be met in a preferential option for the poor. A militant Christian wrote from prison: "Every time I am threatened by bitterness or anguish, I feel the presence of God and all of you supporting me, and then I want only to rejoice."[16] There is a kind of paradoxical "resignation" to joy that is nothing else than the recognition of the strengthening presence of God and the community—a recognition in which our fears, doubts, and discouragement (which are expressions of the "flesh" in the Pauline sense of the term) are routed by the power of the Lord's love.[17]

This is a genuine spiritual combat that follows the model given in a famous and inspiring text of Jeremiah. Like the prophet, many Latin American Christians are frightened by the scope and difficulties of a commitment to the poor and the oppressed. They are experiencing what Paul experienced: "fighting without and fear within" (2 Cor. 7:5). The temptation to withdraw is a continual one in a task that involves confronting the powerful of this world, risking one's life, thwarting the development of talents received, not being able to enjoy times of relaxation and arousing suspicion and rejection even within the Christian community.[18] There are difficult moments in which not a few persons can to some extent make their own the terrible words of Jeremiah:

> Cursed be the day
> on which I was born!
> The day when my mother bore me,
> let it not be blessed!
> Cursed be the man
> who brought the news to my father. . .
> because he did not kill me in the womb
> so my mother would have been my grave,
> and her womb for ever great.
> Why did I come forth from the womb
> to see toil and sorrow,
> and spend my days in shame?
> [Jer. 20:14–15, 17–18].

This passage is an agonized expression of the spiritual struggle I spoke of a moment ago—it is Jacob's struggle with God. The struggle ends, however, in the prophet's loving acknowledgment of God's victory over human cowardice: "You have seduced me, Yahweh, and I have let myself be seduced; you have overpowered me; you were the stronger" (Jer. 20:7, JB). The victory is perhaps not entirely clear, but this does not prevent a trusting, almost "resigned," surrender to the Lord. This struggle, to which there are so many witnesses in the history of spirituality, is making itself felt with new vigor in the experience of Latin American Christians, and it often becomes a collective reality. This happens when an entire people, inspired by its faith and hope, sets out to defend its right to life. On this journey through the desert it experiences failures and the temptation to turn back, but also successes and, above all, hope in the God who liberates and gives life.[19]

We are then in the presence of a people that accepts the exhortation in a recent document of the Chilean bishops: "Despite all the negative signs, we urge you to hope. Hope is an essentially Christian virtue. It is grounded in our certainty that in the death of Jesus Christ God has assumed all our sufferings and failures and that in the resurrection of Jesus God has overcome all evil. In God's hands life is mightier than death."[20]

After the experience of suffering and death, joy comes, and with joy the will that all should have life:

> God has passed through Nicaragua and acted with a mighty and liberating hand. Some signs of that marvelous presence in the midst of our struggling people have been, and continue to be: the hunger of the poor and oppressed for justice, courage, the presence of women, the example of unity, the hospitality and companionship, the sense of responsibility with which the people has taken up its task of reconstruction, and, finally, the generosity shown in victory, and the joy, pregnant with hope, that makes the whole people dream of a better tomorrow for everyone and not just for a few.[21]

From the depth of a happiness that matures in poverty and overcomes suffering, the poor peoples of Latin America are learning, by "the grace of God," like "the churches of Macedonia," how to "overflow in a wealth of liberality" (2 Cor. 8:1–5).

Such is the road of the "new humankind." In one of his poems Bishop Angelelli gives profound expression to what I have been saying:

The mother country is bearing a child
amid blood and pain. . . .
The evenings are shedding tears
for that hope the child may be born
without hatred and with love.
My land is pregnant with life
in this night of pain,
as it waits for dawn to break
and reveal a new person, Lord.[22]

Joy, which in the Bible always accompanies the fulfillment of
the messianic promises (e.g., Isa. 65:17–23), thus recovers its
deepest meaning: that it flows from the conquest of death. "O
death, where is thy victory? O death, where is thy sting?" Paul
asks with joyous mockery in his First Letter to the Corinthians.
Then he emphatically repeats themes already familiar to us: "The
sting of death is sin, and the power of sin is the law." He ends with
thanksgiving for the victory over these manifestations of the
"flesh": "But thanks be to God, who gives us the victory through
our Lord Jesus Christ" (1 Cor. 15:55–57).

9

SPIRITUAL CHILDHOOD:
A REQUIREMENT FOR COMMITMENT
TO THE POOR

A clearsighted and penetrating awareness of the situation of poverty in which the great majorities are living in Latin America has extensively altered the way that the mission of the Latin American church is viewed; it has also brought a great change in Christian commitment. This is especially the case ever since the structural causes of this situation were publicized (e.g., by Medellín and Puebla). A further result is that from the beginning there has been an effort at theological reflection on poverty. Scholars have endeavored to determine the total meaning of the term "poor" in the Bible, in order to show the necessity of a fruitful relationship between material poverty, as it is often called, and spiritual poverty in the following of Jesus, as well as to bring out the ecclesial witness that such a relationship gives.

Interest in this question has not lessened with the passage of time. On the contrary, experience has enriched the approach to the problem and rendered it more acute. Reflection on it has continued and become more profound: the connection between spiritual childhood (in the final analysis, that is what "spiritual poverty" means) and real poverty is central to the spiritual experience that has come into being in Latin America, an area of the world marked by terribly wretched conditions but also a place of great hope.

With the Poor and against Poverty

Puebla made clear the meaning of Christian commitment in this context: "Committed to the poor, we condemn as anti-evangelical the extreme poverty that afflicts an extremely large segment of the population on our continent" (no. 1159). Solidarity with the poor, therefore, and rejection of poverty. Medellín has formulated this approach, in its document, "Poverty," saying that poverty taken on as a commitment "assumes voluntarily and lovingly the condition of the needy of this world, in order to give testimony to the evil that it represents" (no. 4). This focus has since then enriched the practice of the church in Latin America.

This unswerving position has led Christians to see that only in this kind of commitment to the poor is it possible to live spiritual poverty (that is, detachment from the goods of this world) in an authentic way. Testimonies and documents on this point are countless. Spiritual poverty is obligatory for every Christian and for the church as a whole. On this point the members of CLAR (Latin American Conference of Religious) have written:

> We believe that today more than ever before the mission of the church on this continent requires the active presence of religious communities as authentic living sacraments (signs and instruments) of the reign that God exercises in favor of the poor. To this end it is urgent that religious effectively dissociate themselves from the injustices of the prevailing system; that in whatever environment they find themselves they give a clear witness to evangelical poverty by their spirit, their manner of life, and their structures . . . that with evangelical prudence they seek ways of entering into solidarity with the world of the poor in order that they may devote themselves to working therein, through the witness of their life and the service provided by their toil, for the genuine liberation of our peoples in accordance with the spirit of the gospels.[1]

Solidarity with the poor in present-day Latin America is a sure—and quick—way to win the dislike of the privileged and the wealthy. The prevailing social system does not forgive those who are bold enough to follow this path in an authentic manner; it matters not whether they be isolated individuals or the entire ecclesial community. But those who renounce their possessions gain a new realization of the Lord's fidelity. Seeing the repressive measures taken by political authorities against those who try to bear an evangelical witness, the bishops of Guatemala wrote: "In the midst of a merciless struggle that draws the intervention of the mightiest of this world, the church, which is committed to human salvation, finds itself helpless, decimated, powerless, and without refuge, because the only fidelity it acknowledges is fidelity to Christ and its members."[2]

To "remember the poor" (Gal. 2:10) means in Latin America to keep in mind the overwhelming majority of the population. And yet there are not lacking those who misunderstand and resist this option, claiming, for example, that it sets limits to the universal love of God to which the church must bear witness. But, as Bishop Germán Schmitz has said: "If some feel thrust aside by this commitment on the part of the church, it is because they have been unwilling to adopt it along with the church. All those who make it their own will experience the profound joy of knowing that at their side are brothers and sisters who without reservations make this dimension an irreplaceable part of their Christian lives."[3]

Despite this opposition it can be said that in principle a broad consensus exists on the necessity of an authentic commitment of Christians to the situation of poverty in which the Latin American majorities are living. There is also a consensus that without this solidarity detachment from the goods of this world becomes illusory. This conviction has changed the ways in which many persons live poverty.[4]

The World of the Poor

Commitment to the poor is an indispensable requirement for truly living in detachment from material goods.[5] The experience of the Latin American church in recent years has brought to light aspects that were not so clear at the beginning.

As time has passed and there has been an opportunity of drawing up a balance sheet of successes and failures, ambiguities and possibilities, of so many efforts at commitment to the poor and oppressed of Latin America, the enormous complexity of the issue has also become clearer. The solidarity with the poor and the struggle against poverty to which Medellín called us in 1968 are proving to be gigantic tasks. This is not due solely to the strength of the various external resistances that must be overcome; it is due also to the character of the real world in which the poor live.

Beyond any possible doubt, the life of the poor is one of hunger and exploitation, inadequate health care and lack of suitable housing, difficulty in obtaining an education, inadequate wages and unemployment, struggles for their rights, and repression. But that is not all. Being poor is also a way of feeling, knowing, reasoning, making friends, loving, believing, suffering, celebrating, and praying. The poor constitute a world of their own. Commitment to the poor means entering, and in some cases remaining in, that universe with a much clearer awareness; it means being one of its inhabitants, looking upon it as a place of residence and not simply of work. It does not mean going into that world by the hour to bear witness to the gospel, but rather emerging from within it each morning in order to proclaim the good news to every human being.

Contrary to what a certain romantic notion would hold, the world of the poor is not made up simply of victims, of solidarity and the struggle for human rights. The universe of the poor is inhabited by flesh-and-blood human beings, pervaded with the forces of life and death, of grace and sin. In that world we find indifference to others, individualism, abandoned children, people abusing people, pettiness, hearts closed to the action of the Lord. Insofar as the poor are part of human history, they are not free of the motivations found in the two cities of which St. Augustine spoke: love of God and love of self.

But it is also true—and this adds to the complexity—that the specific form these characteristics take bears the mark of an intolerable poverty, of the struggle for basic human survival, of boundary situations. Thus it is often difficult to pronounce definitive judgment with categories belonging to other contexts. This is one more reason to move in this world with the greatest respect.

We see with increasing clarity that it takes a great deal of humility for persons to commit themselves to the poor of our day. In this effort one experiences what Luis Espinal translated into a prayer in which he sought to express the mystery of life:

Lord, a thin drizzle of humility is penetrating us. We are not the axis of life, as our self-centeredness falsely claimed. . . .
We travel through life like blind persons; we did not choose life

before embarking on it, nor do we know the day when we will depart from it. . . . Life is larger than we are, and your ways extend beyond the horizon of our vision.[6]

It will be necessary, therefore, to undertake this commitment although knowing in advance that the situation of the poor will almost certainly overstrain the human capacity for solidarity. The will to live in the world of the poor can therefore only follow an asymptotic curve: a constantly closer approach that can, however, never reach the point of real identification with the life of the poor. Not even the surrender of their lives brings individuals to that goal, despite the ultimacy of the witness they give. Of course, if they have some standing in society or in the Latin American church, their martyrdom will come to be known and honored. This does not in the least detract from the courage and authenticity of their commitment, the profound meaning of which we saw in an earlier section. On the other hand, how can we fail to think of the many rural poor, migrants, women, and workers who have anonymously given their lives for love of their people[7] or simply for having wanted to be there in the midst of the people to celebrate the Lord or to accompany a respected dead person to the grave?[8]

Spiritual Childhood

We should not conclude that commitment to the poor and oppressed, in whose faces we see the suffering features of the Lord, is an impossible undertaking. I am not asking that we be skeptics regarding the possibilities of that kind of solidarity. I wish only to establish that the practice of recent years has made it clear that the approach to the world of the poor must not be accompanied by triumphalism of any kind. Regardless of the intentions at work, triumphalism could lead to a new kind of pharisaism.

I said above that entry into the world of the poor has always demanded a large measure of humility.[9] In fact, that entry can come only as the result of an experience of what the gospel calls childhood. Medellín approaches this matter in a way that is enlightening. It does not present spiritual poverty primarily under the aspect of detachment from material goods; in an approach that is both more profound and more evangelical, it identifies spiritual poverty with spiritual childhood. It is therefore defined as "the attitude of opening up to God, the ready disposition of one who hopes for everything from the Lord," and the church is told that its task is to preach and live "spiritual poverty as an attitude of spiritual childhood and openness to the Lord" ("Poverty," nos. 4-5).

This point is central. Spiritual childhood is one of the most important concepts in the gospel, for it describes the outlook of the person who accepts the gift of divine filiation and responds to it by building fellowship.[10] In part 2 I had occasion to recall the role that these two aspects of Christian existence play in the New Testament.

Such is the attitude to the Lord and to one's neighbor that is required for entering into the world of the poor. It is even something more: an indispensable condition for this solidarity. Only by becoming a child can one enter the kingdom of heaven (Matt. 18:3). The same spiritual childhood is required for entering the world of the poor—those for whom the God of the kingdom has a preferential love.

Perhaps at an earlier time we were more conscious of the relationship that I mentioned a few pages back—namely, that detachment from the goods of this world (which is one aspect of spiritual poverty) can be lived only be taking up one's dwelling in the midst of poverty. That realization is certainly still valid, but to it we must add another and deeper insight: spiritual childhood alone makes possible an authentic commitment to the poor and oppressed.

I do not say this because I enjoy turning formulas on their head. I am talking of an experience shared by many in their search—at once painful and joyous—for God the Father along the ways of the poor.

This spiritual childhood has in Mary, the mother of the Lord, a permanent model. Daughter of a people that put all its trust in God, archetype of those who want to follow the path to the Father, she points out the way. The Magnificat, which Luke places on her lips, gives profound expression to what the practice of Latin American Christians is bringing to light once again in our day.[11] The canticle of Mary combines a trusting self-surrender to God with a will to commitment and close association with God's favorites: the lowly, the hungry.

10

COMMUNITY: OUT OF SOLITUDE

The development of the community dimension of faith is a characteristic of Christian life in our day. Vatican II contributed a great deal to this development. In Latin America one way in which this trend has found expression is in the rise of the basic ecclesial communities, which, in the judgment of Puebla, "are one of the causes for joy and hope in the church" (no. 96).[1] We are also dealing here with another essential aspect of the following of Jesus Christ, as I mentioned when I spoke of the communal experience of encounter with him.

In this section I should like to bring out the fact that for many Latin American Christians this community dimension is not something added simply and with joy to the Christian outlook already in place. In fact, the journey toward life in community frequently takes an unexpected turn: a passage through a painful experience of profound solitude or loneliness.

The experience of the solitude of the desert is a profound aspect of the encounter with God. Passage through this desert is a journey of pure faith, with the support and guidance of God only. In solitude the Lord speaks to us "tenderly" (Hos. 2:14), calls us to fidelity, and consoles us. Being all alone with God, who enriches us with the gift of happiness in the innermost depths of our being, is an ineffable, largely incommunicable, experience. The writings of the great mystics make this very clear.

This experience of solitude is, of course, a classic theme in the history of spirituality, but it has special features in our present situation. It leads to an urgent realization of the importance of the

Christian community, not as a group of which we deign to be a part (as though we might just as well have made the opposite choice), but as a basic ecclesial dimension of walking according to the Spirit.

The Dark Night of Injustice

For those who make the commitment to liberation there is understandably a very keen sense of the situation of the vast majorities, as well as of their role in historical change. In other words, those involved take very seriously the scope of love as expressed in the famous words of M.-D. Chenu: "The masses, my neighbor." This fact, added to what I have just been saying about the community dimension of faith, may lead us to think that there is little room left for the personal dimension, including solitude, in human existence and in the experience of faith. All energies would be poured out into scattered commitment and an unmitigated activism.

There is no doubt that this danger exists. But it is no more than that: a risk; the essential and most fruitful substance of the experience is not to be found there. The passage through what has been called "the dark night" of injustice is part of the spiritual journey in Latin America. On this journey "of an entire people toward its liberation through the desert of structural and organized injustice that surrounds us . . . it is very important to persevere in prayer, even if we hardly do more than stammer groans and cries, while in this struggle the image of God in us is purified in an extraordinary 'dark night.' "[2]

The crossing of the desert takes place only in "a deep and vast wilderness," as John of the Cross said. Many of those who seek to be in solidarity with the poor Latin American masses experience this solitude. There is no authentic acceptance of that commitment that does not involve great difficulties. I know this from the experience of many, and I have been recording the fact in these pages. There are problems with those who see their privileges being challenged; there is isolation due to the new and hitherto unexperienced consequences of assuming the needs of the world of the poor from within; there is distrust and even hostility from many who share the same faith.

However, what renders these difficulties even more intense is the situation of poverty and exploitation in which the poor live. It is a situation that seems to have no end; it is like living halfway through a tunnel. The interests that the poor are challenging, both within each country and at the international level, are very powerful (think of what is happening in Central America in these years). There is, in addition, the great—and unwanted—human cost of an effort at liberation in which no successful outcome can even be glimpsed. It is what García Márquez calls "the immensity of our solitude."[3]

All this gives rise to moments of great suffering and deep loneliness. Juan Alsina, another murdered priest, wrote as follows on the evening before he was found dead:

> We have come to the end of the road; we cut a path but now we are among the rocks . . . we shall continue on, those of us who remain. How long? . . . "None of those who dipped their bread in the fleshpots of Egypt will see the Promised Land without passing through the experience of death." . . . Who is at the other end of the phone? Who is knocking on the door at this hour? The difficulty is not to know what I will do but what they will do, and the most painful question of all: Why? This is the source of the uncertainty and the consciousness of uncertainty, the fear.[4]

Yes, the fear, and why not? The fear not only of dying, which itself is no small matter, but also of weakening, of thinking unduly of oneself. Of beginning to consider other and less costly forms of commitment.

When they find themselves alone—and there are many kinds of solitude—many persons would like to rewrite their lives; they wish they had not done or said this or that. Not all wishes at such a moment are dictated by a healthy self-criticism; weariness plays a part, as does cowardice and even despair at the thought of the many obstacles and misunderstandings that must be overcome. There are also moments for great decisions in which nothing is clear, but a decision must nonetheless be made. There are no fixed points of reference. All that remains is the conviction that one wants to do the Father's will and serve the people, but the moment is so filled with spiritual aridity that despite one's conviction one's tongue cleaves to the roof of one's mouth (Ps. 137:6).

In all these circumstances there is a new encounter with oneself and, above all, a new face-to-face encounter with the Lord who is testing and consoling us. John of the Cross speaks of the "frightful night" through which one must pass, but he also says that the desert is "the more delightful, savorous, and loving, the deeper, vaster, and more solitary it is." Such is the twofold experience of the Christian who wishes to be faithful to the Lord even in the blackest depths of "the dark night of injustice."

Trust in God and in the ecclesial community is present, then, even though the light of day has still not dawned. A Christian militant who made a decision of commitment to his people wrote as follows to his parish priest and friend:

> Brother, neither you nor the community are absent at this moment of irrevocable surrender. I am setting out. Perhaps we shall not see each other again, but I will be present in the struggle and in the community, in the church and in the hills, in the streets and in every word our pastors utter. My greatest desire was that we might have celebrated a Mass together and taken communion together and that you might have forgiven my many sins. I realize that I have not been the best, that I have given little, and that there is a great deal still to be done if we are to see our people free and human beings living together in love of God. Hard though it is, I believe that wherever persons are suffering, it is my Christian duty to bear witness to the Lord and to what we have so often preached: love and community.[5]

These are the unvarnished experiences of followers of the Lord. They are echoes, reverberating down through the history of the Christian community, of the cry of Jesus himself: "My God, my God, why hast thou forsaken me?" (Mark 15:34). But in these experiences Christians do not fail to realize that the deep and rending solitude they feel comes on the threshold of the most tremendous and most radical communion possible: communion in the life and joy of the resurrection.

Living in Community

The passage through the experience of solitude leads to a profound community life. As I have already pointed out, the solitude of which I am speaking is something quite different from individualism. In individualism there is a large measure of withdrawal, at the level of thoughts and interests, in order to ensure a life of quiet privacy. Others may come and knock on the door, but if the individualist opens to them, it is as one who does a favor, as one who graciously adds, so to speak, a community aspect to a Christian life that is self-sufficient without it.

The experience of solitude, on the other hand, gives rise to a hunger for communion. There is an aloneness with oneself and with God that, however hard it may be to endure at certain times, is a requirement for authentic community.

God, in other words, does not call us to the desert to wander endlessly there, but to pass through it, in order to reach the promised land. The journey through the desert creates a community flowing with the milk and honey of the fellowship of those who know God as their Father. There we can sing with the psalmist:

> Behold, how good and pleasant it is
>   when brothers dwell in unity!
> It is like the precious oil upon the head,
>   running down upon the beard,
>   upon the beard of Aaron,
>   running down on the collar of his robes!
> It is like the dew of Hermon,
>   which falls on the mountains of Zion!
> For there the Lord has commanded the blessing,
>   life for evermore [Ps. 133].

There is, however, no question here of two stages: first solitude and *then* community. Rather it is within community that one experiences solitude. The successive levels of depth prove baffling, even to the person who is experiencing them.

This was the experience of Archbishop Romero. His attitude toward solitude and the call to communion are described by Bishop Sergio Méndez Arceo (Cuernavaca, Mexico):

He sought for communion and preached it to others, but he also sought solitude and relinquished it only to confront the enemies of his people. Today this twofold task remains. I can sum up in one phrase his attitude to the call to solitude: good but equivocal. He knew he had to speak to his people, nourish his people.

Brothers and sisters, the task of all of us who are united in his memory is to not abandon him, not permit that he be forgotten. . . . Brothers and sisters, act on this summons: do not let him be forgotten. Do not permit anyone to isolate him. He died in behalf of the people, for the people—that is, he died in behalf of God, for God. Our work is a Christian work in the service of the God of Jesus Christ. It is not opposition to anyone; it is service.[6]

The support of the community is essential for the crossing of the desert. So true is this that only in community can one travel this road. According to basic ecclesial communities in Brazil:

The faith and courage of the members of our communities in the face of threats, misunderstandings, and persecution for justice' sake are sustained and strengthened by the support each individual gives the others, by the support each community gives the others, by our very struggle and activity, by meditation on the word of God, and by the recollection of the witness given by those who have struggled for justice.[7]

Community life cultivates receptivity for God's reign and also proclaims it; in this reception and proclamation a community builds itself up as a community. "Only in community can we hear, accept, and proclaim the gift and grace of the Lord, the special call to overcome everything that destroys comradely communion (oppression, injustice, marginalization, discrimination, etc.)—because at the same time it destroys communion with God—and to struggle for the values of the kingdom that Jesus proclaimed."[8]

The community is also the place where we remember the death and resurrection of the Lord. In part 2 I remarked on the realism with which Paul speaks of our membership in the body of Christ. It implies liberation of our own bodies from the forces of death: sin, the root of all injustice. Against the background of the poverty and exploitation in which the majority of Latin Americans

live, against the background of their emaciated, sometimes mas-
sacred, bodies, the Spirit deepens in us the meaning of the Eucharist as an act of thanksgiving to the Father for sharing with us
the body of the dead and resurrected Christ.

The breaking of the bread is at once the point of departure and
the point of arrival of the Christian community. In it is expressed
profound communion in human sorrow and joyous acknowledgment of the risen Savior who gives life to and raises the hope of
those assembled in *ecclesia* by his words and deeds.

It is in the eucharistic community that hope in the Lord is fed:

> The Eucharist, or the Supper of the Lord, should hold the cen-
> tral place in our communities, together with the sharing of the
> word of God. When they are celebrated among the poor and
> oppressed, they are both a promise and demand of justice, of
> the freedom and the fellowship for which the peoples of the
> Third World are struggling.[9]

Many persons have experienced the depth and creativity of celebrations among the people. To a firm conviction of faith that is
rooted in an ecclesial and personal tradition there is added an
increasingly clear realization that the Eucharist celebrates a hope.
The act of thanksgiving that is the Eucharist expresses a confidence that the communion of life that does not yet exist among us
can become a reality. This "anticipation," if I may so put it, is not
an evasion; rather it motivates a present commitment. It represents an acknowledgment that the gift of life given by the risen
Christ concerns every moment and every area of human existence.

This celebration is carried out in community—but a community that extends beyond the confines of the near and the local,
because it is both the expression and the task of the entire church.
As Rutilio Grande once put it:

> This morning, here in Apopa, the several parish communities
> here represented are not present as a sect cut off either from the
> local church or from the universal church. We feel ourselves
> part of the church, which we love and want to see continually
> renewed by the power of the Holy Spirit . . . in the midst of the
> world and its problems. We love the church not simply in the

light of what it ought to be but as it now is, with its need of continual conversion.[10]

In the church we experience moments of solitude as well as times of community sharing.[11] We are a messianic people on pilgrimage through history and we are, of course, exposed to the vicissitudes of that process in its varied forms; nonetheless it is in and with the people that we go our way. The ecclesial outlook is one of the dominant notes of the spirituality now coming to birth in Latin America.

"In the end, Lord, I die a daughter of the church," said the great Teresa of Avila, a woman who had to endure a great deal of painful misunderstanding in her lifetime, even in her final years.[12] It is in the church, the historical sacrament of the kingdom of life, that the committed Christians of Latin America are living—and dying.

CONCLUSION

In the midst of many and varied forms of suffering something new is being born in Latin America. This is what prompts talk of a *kairos*, a favorable time—a moment when the Lord knocks on the doors of the ecclesial community that lives in Latin America and asks it to open to him so that he may come and dine there (Rev. 3:20).

Discourse on faith is a second stage in relation to the life of faith itself. This methodological statement is a central one in the theology of liberation. But the statement does not imply a separation of the two stages or aspects. Its point is simply to emphasize the fact that authentic theological reflection has its basis in contemplation and in practice. Talk about God (theo-logy) comes after the silence of prayer and after commitment. Theology is discourse that is continually enriched by silence. It is a discourse that sinks its roots into a faith lived in ecclesial communion and thus grafted into a history of the transmission and acceptance of the Christian message.

When looked at in this way, the (very traditional) distinction between first act and second act is not operative solely in what is commonly understood as the area of theological methodology. Rather it reflects a way of living the faith; it has to do with the following of Jesus. As a matter of fact, our methodology is our spirituality. There is nothing surprising about this. After all, the word "method" comes from *hodos*, "way." Reflection on the mystery of God (for that is what a theology is) is possible only in the context of the following of Jesus. Only when one is walking according to the Spirit can one think and proclaim the gratuitous love of the Father for every human being.

My aim in these pages has been to reflect on the experience of "walking" that is going on today in Latin America, the experience of the road to holiness—to use a term not often mentioned in discussion of such difficult and controversial contexts as ours. I am convinced, nonetheless, of the universality and urgency of the call of Jesus: "You, therefore, must be perfect, as your heavenly Father is perfect" (Matt. 5:48). In addition, I think that in the final analysis only holiness can certify, and render binding on the entire church, the testimony of those who are trying to express their faith and hope through solidarity with, and love for, the poor and oppressed of Latin America—those who thus express their option for life.

Spirituality is a community enterprise. It is the passage of a people through the solitude and dangers of the desert, as it carves out its own way in the following of Jesus Christ. This spiritual experience is the well from which we must drink. From it we draw the promise of resurrection.

NOTES

Introduction

1. See the section entitled "A Spirituality of Liberation" in G. Gutiérrez, *A Theology of Liberation* (Maryknoll, N.Y.: Orbis, 1972), pp. 203–8. Ever since I published that book I have been intending to develop the theme of those pages more fully. Only now has it been possible for me to do so; the delay has the advantage that I can now draw on the experiences and reflections of so many others in recent years. In satisfying this long overdue obligation to myself, I shall necessarily be making frequent references back to that earlier sketch of the subject, and for this I apologize to the reader.

2. This point has been studied in fruitful books that are evidence of the importance of this theme in Latin America. A. Paoli, *Freedom to Be Free* (Maryknoll, N.Y.: Orbis, 1973); Cardinal E. Pironio, *Reflexiones sobre el hombre nuevo en América Latina* (Buenos Aires: Patria Grande, 1974); S. Galilea, *Espiritualidad de la liberación* (Santiago de Chile: ISPAJ, 1974); J. B. Libânio, *Spiritual Discernment and Politics: Guidelines for Religious Communities* (Maryknoll, N.Y.: Orbis, 1982); J. Sobrino, "The Following of Jesus as Discernment," in *Concilium*, 119 (1979) 14–24; various authors, *Espiritualidad de la liberación* (Lima: CEP, 1980); N. Zevallos, *Espiritualidad del desierto. Espiritualidad de la inserción* (Bogotá: Indo-American Press, 1981); L. Boff, *Vida segundo o espíritu* (Petrópolis: Vozes, 1982); various authors, *Espiritualidad y liberación en América Latina* (San José, Costa Rica: DEI, 1982).

3. E.g., *Irruption of the Third World: Challenge to Theology,* Virginia Fabella and Sergio Torres, eds. (Maryknoll, N.Y.: Orbis, 1983).

4. St. Bernard of Clairvaux, *De consideratione libri quinque ad Eugenium tertium*, II, 1, 2; Migne, P.L., CLXXXII, 745D; cited in E. Gilson, *Théologie et histoire de la spiritualité* (Paris: Vrin, 1943), p. 20.

5. The present book contains the talks given at the XII Jornadas de Reflexión Teológica (1982), organized by the theology department of the Pontifical Catholic University of Peru. They are the fruit of studies done in the Instituto Bartolomé de Las Casas. I thank its staff for their help. I have published a short article with the same title as the present book in *Concilium*, 159 (1982) 38–45, and in *Páginas*, no. 47 (1982).

Part One

Chapter 1

1. "Sobre el proyecto de Verrettes" (Feb. 25, 1983), in *Haití. Opresión y resistencia. Testimonios de cristianos* (Lima: CEP, 1983), pp. 97–98.—The idea that land was a source of fertility was very strong in Andean culture: "The earth is the mother—*pachamama*—that gives food to human beings, gives them life. They disappear into it at death. Before digging the first furrow in a field, the pardon is begged and a blessing is offered, that the harvest may be plentiful" (Luis Dalle, *Antropología y evangelización desde el runa* [Lima: CEP, 1983], p. 98).

2. I shall not develop this point here, because I have dealt with it in detail in other books; see *A Theology of Liberation*, chap. 6: "The Process of Liberation in Latin America," and *The Power of the Poor in History: Selected Writings* (Maryknoll, N.Y.: Orbis, 1983), pp. 77–90.

3. A character of Arguedas in *El zorro de arriba y el zorro de abajo* exclaims at the poverty of the Chimbotan people: "Death in one's native land of Peru is a foreigner. . . . Life, too, is a foreigner."

4. One aspect of this breakthrough is described as follows in the Puebla Document: "From the depths of the countries making up Latin America a cry is rising to heaven, growing louder and more alarming all the time. It is the cry of a suffering people who demand justice, freedom, and respect for the basic rights of human beings and peoples" (no. 87).

5. This is the central theme in F. Guamán Poma de Ayala's *El primer nueva corónica y buen gobierno* (Mexico City: Siglo XXI, 1980), 3 vols. See also Juan Ossio, "Guamán Poma: Nueva corónica o carta al rey. Un intento de aproximación a las categorías del pensamiento andino," in *Ideología mesiánica del mundo andino* (Lima, 1973), pp. 153–207. The establishment of a just world demands the radical inversion of the present situation.

6. See below, part 2, chap. 5.

7. A group of Christians expelled from Olancho, Honduras, wrote to the relatives of *campesinos,* teachers, and priests who had been assassinated in Olancho: "Now we have shared the same persecution expressed in unending criticisms, false accusations, insults, arbitrary arrests, plunderings, pressures, threats, lack of control over and uncertainty about the future, problems in making oneself understood, etc. We are proud to be identified with you, especially now that two more of our brothers in the priesthood have undergone the same fate, under the same circumstances" (priests, religious, and lay persons expelled from Olancho, "Carta a familiares de las víctimas" [March 22, 1975], in SLE, p. 242).

8. As regards the situation in Haiti, which in one way or another is paralleled in many other parts of Latin America, the following has been stated: "We do not think that the exodus of Haitian refuges derives from purely economic causes. It derives principally from the dynastic and lifelong regimen of J.C. Duvalier, who is the lord and master of the Haitian people, with the backing of a privileged minority and the brute force of the dreaded Macoutes, denying to the Haitian people the most elementary human rights" (statement of the Conference of Religious of Puerto Rico, March 26, 1982, in *Haití*, p. 99).

9. For the life and work of Oscar Romero, see the excellent book by James R. Brockman, *The Word Remains: A Life of Oscar Romero* (Maryknoll, N.Y.: Orbis, 1982). For an analysis of the theological and pastoral significance of his witness, see Jon Sobrino, *Oscar Romero, profeta mártir de la liberación* (Lima: CEP, 1981).

10. Some may be tempted to think of this spirituality as traditional, but the validity of the judgment depends on the period assigned for the beginning of the tradition. I think that this idea is too important and meaningful in Christian experience to be employed in reference to what follows.

11. It should be remembered, however, that St. Francis de Sales took an important step in addressing his *Introduction to the Devout Life* to the laity of his time.

12. One of the most influential theologians in this area was Yves Congar; see, in this context, his *Lay People in the Church: A Study for a Theology of the Laity* (Westminster, Md.: Newman, 1957), especially chap. 9: "In the World and Not of the World."

13. See C. Leonardi, "From 'Monastic' Holiness to 'Political' Holiness," in *Concilium*, 149 (1979) 46: "For many centuries the model of holiness was the monk. From the fourth to the twentieth century Christians thought of the perfect imitation of Christ as the monastic life, but now this image is worn out." But there is a point to be made that may necessitate a rethinking of this relationship. In the beginning, monastic spirituality was a way of continuing the spirituality of martyrdom; see Louis Bouyer, *The Spirituality of the New Testament and the Fathers* (History of Christian Spirituality 1; New York: Desclee, 1963), pp. 190–210. We may therefore ask whether the age of martyrdom that we are now experiencing in Latin America (to be developed further on in this book) does not establish a new connection (though in a different context) between the nascent spiritual experience of today, which many lay persons are now having, and the spirituality of the martyrs in the early centuries, which was the source of monastic spirituality.

14. CLAR (Latin American Conference of Religious) has stated: "Many religious, men and women, realize with dismay that their life in community is far removed from that of the poor in their environs. If the religious commu-

nity lives in comfort, not only is it difficult for its members to exercise poverty, but they distance themselves objectively from the people, millions of whom live in shacks made from cardboard boxes or sheets of tin, in the worst possible hygienic and moral conditions, lacking even bread on a daily basis" (*Pobreza y vida religiosa en América Latina* [Bogotá: CLAR, 1970], p. 25).

15. As the bishops said at Puebla: "A preferential option for the poor represent[s] the most notable tendency of religious life in Latin America" (no. 733); and: "This has led to a reexamination of traditional works in order to respond better to the demands of evangelization. It has also shed clearer light on their relationship with the poverty of the marginalized. Now this does not imply simply interior detachment and community austerity; it also implies solidarity with the poor, sharing with them, and in some cases living alongside them" (no. 734; cf. Medellín, "Religious" nos. 7–8). Years earlier the religious of CLAR had written: "In order to give concrete form to this service and at the same time ensure its continuity, the religious communities that the Spirit has raised up in the people of God have had to find adequate institutional structures. Throughout history, it has been possible for these structures, like those of any institution, to forget that they are only means in the service of the love that the community is called upon to offer the people. In a world such as ours here in Latin America, in which socio-economic and cultural change is so rapid and so profound, it is to be expected that these structures risk becoming unsuitable and even reaching the point, without realizing it, where they contradict the very mission of witness and effective service that is the reason for the existence of the communities as well as their original charismatic inspiration" (*Pobreza y vida religiosa,* p. 52; cf. p. 66). See also *La vida según el Espíritu en las comunidades religiosas de América Latina* (Bogotá: CLAR, 1973), p. 61. These considerations had led to a vigorous renewal of religious life in Latin America.

16. This is the title of a now classic work of its kind: J. Tissot, *The Interior Life Simplified and Reduced to Its Fundamental Principle* (Westminster, Md.: Newman, 2nd ed., 1949; the French original dates from 1894). This manual was widely used in seminaries and houses of formation.

17. After pointing out the necessity of paying attention to both "personal structures" and "social structures" in spirituality, because "no theological reasoning can justify their separation," Pedro Arrupe explains why the social dimension came to be neglected: "As it seems to me, the only explanation of this neglect, in traditional ascesis and spirituality, is that Christians were aware, to a greater or lesser degree (and Christianity itself heightened this awareness), that they could change themselves by themselves. . . . By contrast, it is only in more recent times that we have become aware that the world in which we live, together with its structures, its organization, its ideas, its

systems, and so forth . . . are also changeable, reformable. . . . The structures of this world—customs, social, economic, and political systems, commercial relationships, and, in general, all the institutions that humankind has created—to the extent that they incorporate injustice, are the concrete forms in which sin has been objectified." This leads him to an important and thought-provoking idea: structures marked by sin can be given the Johannine designation "world." "If the concept of the world was not developed in theology as the concept of concupiscence was, this was because in the past too much attention was paid to the purely individual dimension. Now that we have overcome that false emphasis, we must apply to the concept 'world' the same theological constructs that have been elaborated on the concept 'concupiscence,' so that it can realize all its forceful dynamism. The world is for the social dimension what concupiscence is for the individual" (address to the tenth international congress of alumni of Jesuit universities, Valencia, July 31, 1973, in *Vie chrétienne*, 178 [June 1975] 6–7).

18. This outlook can lead to unbelievable extremes. A humorous but revealing example may be found in a book on spirituality entitled *Comment eviter le Purgatoire* ("how to avoid purgatory"), published in France at the end of the eighteenth century. The book lists ten means of achieving the objective, one of them being "to elicit an act of charity, at least once every five years." At least. . . ! Although Tissot's book (see n. 16, above) does not go that far, it does not contain any extended discussion of charity as love of God and neighbor. In fact, our relationship with our neighbor plays no part in the spiritual journey as presented by Tissot. It must be acknowledged that the work, at one time much celebrated, of G. Gilleman, *The Primacy of Charity in Moral Theology* (Westminster, Md.: Newman, 1959), had the great merit of restoring the long absent perspective of charity to Christian thinking about human action. (See also R. Aubert, *La théologie catholique du milieu du XX siècle* [Paris: Casterman, 1954], p. 79; G. Thils, *Orientations de la théologie* [Louvain: Centerik, 1958]). Our thanks, then, to G. Gilleman—but how are we to explain the theological eclipse of that behavioral norm that is the most important of all for the follower of him who left us "a new commandment" (John 15:12), and, in the Thomistic pespective, played the role of "the form of all the other virtues"? In his classic and richly detailed book, *Leçons de théologie spirituelle* (Toulouse: Editions de la Revue d'Ascétique et de Mystique, 1955), J. de Guibert asserts the primacy of charity in the spiritual life and shows that this notion has strong patristic support (see esp. pp. 137–47). Nevertheless his book does not explore in depth the connection between love of God and love of neighbor as a key element in Christian spirituality.

19. To be sure, I am not denying the significance of attitudes such as pride and humility from the human and Christian standpoints; I am referring only to the spiritualist reductionism that is sometimes found.

20. Archbishop Carlos Partelli of Montevideo writes pointedly: "The encounter with Jesus Christ leads by itself to a summons to break off an individualistic lifestyle. To follow him means a new way of living-with, sharing-with, committing oneself to, the lowly" ("Carta Pastoral," Montevideo, 1978, p. 25).

21. See J. C. Guy, *Saint Ignace de Loyola: Exercises spirituels* (Paris: Seuil, 1982), p. 43: "The key question that every school of spirituality must answer is how to reconcile presence to the world with presence to God, or however you prefer to formulate it. How are we to overcome the duality and interrelate the two presences? This question runs through the history of spirituality." As a matter of fact, Ignatian spirituality is one of the most notable and fruitful of the successful efforts for a synthesis.

Chapter 2

1. Some of the ideas in this section have alrady been presented in my "Fidelidad a la vida," in the collection of essays entitled *Signos de vida y fidelidad* (SVF) (Lima: CEP, 1983), pp. 17–22.

2. In part 3 I shall try to specify the meaning and spiritual roots of this attitude.

3. With a pastoral fondness Bishop Valencia Cano sings of this solidarity among the poor in one of his poems: "And my impoverished people, looking for ways to earn another centavo to help me help my impoverished people!" (*Con Dios a la madrugada* [Bogotá: Tercer Mundo, 1965], p. 38).

4. Medellín presented this demand for solidarity with the poor as a demand made of every Christian. In his encyclical on human work John Paul II reminded us of the fact that the church is being faithful to the Lord when it commits itself to solidarity with the movements in which workers claim their basic rights. Here is the final part of this important passage: "In order to achieve social justice in the various parts of the world, in the various countries and in the relationships between them, there is a need for ever *new movements of solidarity of* the workers *and with* the workers. This solidarity must be present whenever it is called for by the social degrading of the subject of work, by exploitation of the workers, and by the growing areas of poverty and even hunger. The church is firmly committed to this cause and considers it its mission, its service, a proof of its fidelity to Christ, so that it can truly be the 'church of the poor' " (*The Pope Speaks*, 26 [1981]: 302). For a theological commentary on this text, see G. Gutiérrez, "El Evangelio del trabajo," in *Sobre el trabajo humano* (Lima: CEP, 1982), pp. 11–63.

5. Incredible though it seems, the reality of poverty in its various forms is denied, openly or indirectly, by some in Latin America. A few years ago, I heard the following story from a Salvadoran *campesino*. A delegation of

rural poor brought their problems to a high political official (I cannot recall whether it was a minister or the president of the republic himself). When one of them spoke of a measure being taken that was injurious to native cultural traditions, the dignitary in question interrupted him and said: "Here in El Salvador there is no Indian population." In response the speaker continued his petition in an indigenous tongue, one that the politician certainly did not understand.

6. To tell the truth, such incidents have occurred ever since the beginning of the evangelization of what were then called the Indies. At that time, it is clear, those who proclaimed the Christian message defended the rights of the poor and challenged the power of the ruling class. This power was represented at the time by the *encomenderos*, "agents," "commissioners." A notable case was the assassination of Antonio Valdivieso, bishop of what is now Nicaragua. Here is the story of his murder: "It happened that while preaching in behalf of the freedom of the Indians he reproached the conquistadors and governors for their ill treatment of the Indians. They grew angry at him and let him know it by their words and actions. . . . Among the soldiers who had come from Peru because they were dissatisfied there was one Juan Bermejo, a man of evil mind. He joined the party of the Contreras brothers, one of whom was governor of Nicaragua. . . . He went out with some companions . . . and went to the house of the bishop, whom he found there with his companion Fray Alonso and another virtuous cleric, and, casting off all respect for what is sacred, stabbed him" (Gil Gonzáles Dávila, *Teatro eclesiástico de la primitiva iglesia de las Indias Occidentales*, vol. 1, pp. 235–36, cited in E. Dussel, *El Episcopado latinoamericano y la liberación de los pobres, 1504–1620* [Mexico City: Centro de Reflexión Teológica, 1979], pp. 335–36).

7. See *A Theology of Liberation*, p. 136. One of the first assassinated was Henrique Pereira Neto, a young black priest and collaborator of Dom Hélder Câmara in Recife, Brazil. A close friend of mine, I dedicated *A Theology of Liberation* to him.

8. See the poem that Bishop Pedro Casaldáliga wrote on the murder of Archbishop Oscar Romero:

> The angel of the Lord declared in the evening . . .
> The heart of El Salvador took note
> Of the 24th, of March and of agony.
> You were offering up the Bread,
>   the living Body. . . .
> Latin America has already set you
>   with all the glory of Bernini
> In the halo-foam of its seas,
> In the age-old altarpiece of the Andes,

> In the wrathful canopy of all its forests,
> In the song of all its pathways,
> In the new Calvary of all its prisons,
>   all its trenches,
>   all its altars,
> And the secure altar of its children's sleepless heart!
> St. Romero of America, our pastor and martyr,
> No one will silence your final Homily!

(cited in T. Cabestrero, *Mystic of Liberation: A Portrait of Pedro Casaldá-liga* [Maryknoll, N.Y.: Orbis, 1981], pp. 191-92).

9. See the documentation presented by Martin Lange and Reinhold Iblacker, eds., in *Witnesses of Hope* (Maryknoll, N.Y.: Orbis, 1981). Karl Rahner writes in the Foreword: "The book narrates martyrdoms in the strict theological sense of the term. . . . There is no suggestion made here that every episode narrated in this book by itself clearly and fully realizes the concept of martyrdom in the theological sense of the term. But, all in all, true martyr-doms are narrated here: in the world of today, they have the significance and function of a witnessing to the supernatural mission of the church, and that is what Christian theology in the era of the primitive church acknowledged to be martyrdom. . . . This book bears testimony to an authentic theology of liber-ation. After reading this book can the reader still reject the theology of libera-tion *en gros* as an exercise in modern secularism? Or must not the reader admit that the *Sitz im Leben*, the point of departure, of this theology is legiti-mate because it gets a footing at a spot from which leads a path that goes all the way to the end—when persons sacrifice their lives for their fellows? Does the book not reveal a theology of liberation that is lived experience, non-violent, not evocative of *ars gratia artis*, but showing that it knows well how to shoulder responsibility for the poor and needy?" (pp. xiv-xv).

10. See L. Bouyer, *The Spirituality of the New Testament and the Fathers* (New York: Desclee, 1963), p. 190: "The importance of martyrdom in the spirituality of the early church would be difficult to exaggerate. But it did not have this exceptional importance merely for the particular period when the majority of martyrdoms took place. After the elements of the New Testa-ment, certainly no other factor has had more influence in constituting Chris-tian spirituality."

11. "Today we are living through an important and difficult moment in that process [of evangelization]" (PD, no. 342).

12. "In this new situation my outlook continues to be a pastoral one; my aim is to encourage a hope that I honestly glimpse. My work has always been to support the hope of my people. If there is even a spark of hope, it is my duty to nourish it, and I believe that every person of good will must likewise nour-

ish it'' (homily of Nov. 11, 1979). I cite Archbishop Romero's homilies from the complete texts that have been appearing in the Salvadoran periodical *Sentir con la Iglesia*, but I shall give only the dates of the homilies.

13. See the historical study by M. Mollat, *Les Pauvres au moyen age* (Paris: Etudes Sociales, 1979).

14. See M. Gelabert and J. M. Milagro, *Santo Domingo de Guzmán, visto por sus contemporáneos* (Madrid: Biblioteca de Autores Cristianos, 1947), and the beautiful book of L. Boff, *Saint Francis: A Model for Human Liberation* (New York: Crossroad, 1982).

15. "La Soledad de América Latina," *Páginas*, 51 (Feb. 1983): 28.

16. This, as readers probably know, is one of the earliest insights gained by the theology of liberation; see the reflections on integral liberation in my *A Theology of Liberation*, pp. 36-37, 143-44.

17. "Human solidarity at the most difficult moments of history is a revealing sign of the love that does not die, because it is identical with *life* itself, and life remains forever, strengthening the powerless and guiding those who trust in the God who promises liberation. Our people is proclaiming to us today this mysterious stubbornness of those who hope against all hope, those who remain unshakably convinced of the justice of their cause and of the power of truth to change history. Their struggle keeps this hope from being smothered and causes it to reach everyone, in order to rouse us all to the *defense of life*" (ONIS, "Situación del pueblo y responsabilidad cristiana," in *Signos de lucha y esperanza* [SLE] [Lima: CEP, 1978], p. 38, italics added).

18. Archbishop Romero put it clearly: "We believe in Jesus who came to bring life in its fulness, and we believe in a God who gives life to human beings and wants them truly to live. These radical truths of faith really become truths, and radical truths, when the church takes its place amid the life and death of its people. Here the church, like every human being, is faced with the choice that is most fundamental for its faith: to be on the side of life or on the side of death. We see very clearly that on this point no neutrality is possible. Either we serve the life of the Salvadoran people or we connive in their death. Here, too, is the historical mediation of what is most fundamental in the Christian faith: either we believe in a God of life or we serve the idols of death" (Address at Louvain, Feb. 2, 1980; in SVF, p. 373). English translation, Orbis Books, forthcoming.

19. This is the proviso for the following of Jesus in an ecclesial framework. Hugo Echegaray was weighing his words carefully when he wrote: "Christian militants are faced with the problem of determining what it means to say that they are to prolong the practice of Jesus. The question can be answered only in terms of the following of Christ—that is, of effective discipleship. It is essential for Christians of every generation that they be able to decide what this following consists in and what it concretely entails if it is to unify their

lives. If these questions are not answered, the spiritual experience of believers will develop on the periphery of the church" (*La práctica de Jesús* [Lima: CEP, 1980], p. 57). English translation, *The Practice of Jesus* (Maryknoll, N.Y.: Orbis Books, 1984).

20. "I am going to speak to you simply as a pastor who, along with his people, has been learning a beautiful and harsh truth: that the Christian faith does not separate us from the world but immerses us in it; that the church, therefore, is not a fortress set apart from the city, but a follower of the Jesus who lived, worked, struggled, and died in the midst of the city" (Address at Louvain, in SVF, p. 367b).

21. Statement to José Calderón Salazar, correspondent for the daily *Excelsior* of Mexico City, published in *Orientación* (San Salvador), April 13, 1980. English translation from Plácido Erdozaín, *Archbishop Romero: Martyr of Salvador* (Maryknoll, N.Y.: Orbis, 1981), p. 75.

Part Two

Chapter 3

1. The theme of an experiential christology in Mark has been deepened by the recent work of Edward Schillebeeckx.

2. Many years ago, in a well-known book that was much misunderstood at the time, M.-D. Chenu wrote as follows about doing theology: "The fact is that in the final analysis theological systems are simply the expressions of a spirituality. It is this that gives them their interest and grandeur. If we are surprised by the theological divergences found within the unity of dogma, then we must also be surprised at seeing one and the same faith give rise to such varied spiritualities. The grandeur and truth of Bonaventuran and Scotist Augustinianism is entirely derived from the spiritual experience of St. Francis, which inspired his sons; the grandeur and truth of Molinism derives from the spiritual experience of the *Exercises* of St. Ignatius. One does not get to the heart of a system via the logical coherence of its structure or the plausibility of its conclusions. One gets to that heart by grasping it in its origins via that fundamental intuition that serves to guide a spiritual life and provides the intellectual regimen proper to that life" (*Le Saulchoir: Una scuola di teologia* [Casale Monferrato: Marietti, 1982], p. 59; the French original dates from 1937).

3. *Proslogion* 1, *Anselm of Canterbury* (New York: Edwin Mellon Press, 1974), vol. 1, p. 93.

4. "In the early centuries of the church, what we now term theology was closely linked to the spiritual life. It was essentially a meditation on the Bible, geared toward spiritual growth" (G. Gutiérrez, *A Theology of Liberation*, p. 4).

5. See Y. Congar, "Théologie," DTC, 15:346–447; and J. Comblin, *Historia da teología católica* (São Paulo: Herder, 1969).

6. Despite his somewhat anti-intellectual bias, Thomas à Kempis is right when he warns: "If we desire to have a true understanding of His Gospels, we must study to conform our life as nearly as we can to His. What avails it to a man to reason about the high, secret mysteries of the Trinity if he lack humility and so displeases the Trinity?" (*Imitation of Christ*, book 1, chap. 1, Richard Whitford, trans. [1530] [Garden City, N.Y.: Doubleday, 1955], p. 31).

7. This is a way of saying that one function of theology is reflection, in the light of faith, on the basis of and about practice. Spirituality is in fact located on the terrain of practice, the terrain of Christian experience.

8. The passage in John continues: "Now this he said about the Spirit, which those who believed in him were to receive." See the analysis of I. de la Potterie, "Parole et Esprit dans S. Jean," in M. De Jonge, ed., *L'Evangile de Jean. Sources, rédaction, théologie* (Gembloux: Duculot, 1977), pp. 177–201. More recently: J. Caba, "Jn. 7, 37–39 en la teología del IV Evangelio sobre la oración de petición," *Gregorianum*, 63 (1982): 647–75.

9. A key issue in the "Johannine Question" is the identity of the author of this Gospel. Many today tend to think that authorship should be assigned to the "beloved disciple" (who would be the person not mentioned by name in the passage cited), but that one or more of his own disciples wrote the Gospel on the basis of the beloved disciple's testimony. On the distinction between author and writer, see M. E. Boismard and E. Cathenet, *La tradition johannique*, vol. 4 in A. George and P. Grelot, eds., *Introduction à la Bible* (Paris: Desclée, 1977), pp. 269–92. The beloved disciple, as traditionally thought, John the son of Zebedee (ibid., 288–90), may be the historical source of the fourth Gospel—including passages of the evangelist himself, according to Oscar Cullmann (*The Johannine Circle* [Philadelphia: Westminster, 1976])—or, as R. E. Brown holds (abandoning his earlier position), he may not be one of the Twelve at all (see *The Community of the Beloved Disciple* [New York: Paulist, 1979], pp. 33–34).

10. J. Mateos and J. Barreto, *El Evangelio de Juan* (Madrid: Cristiandad, 1979), p. 103.

11. For a study of the theme of discipleship in the Gospel of Matthew, see the excellent book of J. Zumstein, *La condition du croyant dans l'évangile selon Matthieu* (Fribourg: Editions Universitaires; Göttingen: Vandenhoeck u. Ruprecht, 1977). For the Gospel of Mark, and particularly for the christological function of "walking the terrain" of Jesus, with its consequences for the path of the disciple, see E. Manicardi, *Il cammino de Gesú nel Vangelo di Marco* (Rome: Biblical Institute, 1981).

12. The text literally says rather that "they stayed with him that day." I am

here adopting the translation of the *Nueva Biblia española;* see the explanation in Mateos and Barreto, *Evangelio,* p. 115, which I find satisfactory.

13. Symbolical interpretations of the hour mentioned are not lacking. The tenth hour (tenth of the twelve into which the day was divided between sunrise and sunset; 4 P.M. for us) is supposed, for example, to signify the end of the period of the old Israel and the announcement of the new day (Mateos and Barreto, ibid., p. 118). Others maintain, for sound reasons, that the mention of the hour "can hardly have a symbolic meaning" (R. Schnackenburg, *The Gospel according to St. John* [New York: Herder & Herder, 1968], vol. 1, p. 309).

14. Between the question of the disciples and the answer of Jesus, Luke interpolates cures that confirm the point made in the text of Isaiah: "In that hour he cured many of diseases and plagues and evil spirits, and on many that were blind he bestowed sight" (Luke 7:21). This interpolation leads Luke to invert the word order in Jesus' answer as compared with the answer in Matthew: "Go and tell John what you have *seen* and heard" (7:22).

15. John Paul II, encyclical *Rich in Mercy,* no. 3.

16. See J. Dupont, "Jésus annonce la bonne nouvelle aux pauvres," in *Evangelizare pauperibus* (Atti della XXIV Settimana Biblica; Brescia: Paideia, 1978), p. 183: "The proclamation of the good news is *not something* different from the cures of the sick; it is the formula that generalizes and makes explicit the meaning of those cures. The fact that a certain number of sick persons find health in a miraculous manner becomes good news for all the afflicted and a reason to hope for the end of their suffering." And, as he finishes his commentary on the texts I have been discussing, Dupont makes this strong statement: "One thing is certain in any case: the good news proclaimed to the poor *can be naught else than the news that they will cease to be poor* and to suffer poverty. Just as the blind see and the deaf hear and the dead are restored to life, so the poor will not lack what they need; they will cease to be victims of an unjust distribution of goods" [italics added].

17. See the classic work by G. Minette de Tillesse, *Le secret messianique dans l'Evangile de Marc* (Paris: Cerf, 1968), which gives a detailed account of the state of the question on the interpretation of Mark's Gospel launched by W. Wrede at the beginning of the twentieth century.

18. It is interesting that Mark sites this dialogue in Caesarea Philippi, near pagan territories.

19. Let it be noted in passing that John the Baptist, a contemporary of Jesus and his disciples, must have left a very deep impression: some thought he may have returned to life.

20. The same appears again in Mark 6:14-16, as noted by V. Taylor, *The Gospel according to St. Mark* (London: MacMillan, 1953), p. 376.

21. Luke adds "of God" (9:20). Stressing his divinity more explicitly, Mat-

thew says "the Son of the living God" (16:16). This is a profession of faith that could have been made only because the Father so revealed it, as Matthew, always attentive to such details, points out (16:17).

22. The reason for the "messianic secret" is disputed. Minette de Tillesse, at the end of a painstaking study, writes: "The messianic secret is not a reflection of Jesus' pedagogical preoccupation to inculcate in his disciples a more spiritual notion of the Messiah, in opposition to a political notion, as he repeated many times and with care. The end point that he assigns to this secret—'until the Son of Man is risen'—refutes this opinion" (*Le secret messianique*, p. 321).

23. The Vulgate reads: "*Vade retro me*." The Greek word *opiso* is used in formulas having to do with the following of Jesus—e.g., Matt. 8:34, literally: "if anyone wants to follow behind me *(opiso mou akolouthein)*." See M. J. Lagrange, *L'Evangile selon saint Marc* (Paris: Gabalda, 1942), p. 219. See also *Nouveau Testament* (Traduction oecuménique de la Bible, Paris: Cerf, 1975), the note on Mark 8:33 (p. 156).

24. *A Theology of Liberation*, pp. 283–95.

25. Minette de Tillesse writes: "The object of the messianic secret is not the fact of Jesus' messiahship: if it were, Peter's confession would have put an end to it. It is more exactly the 'how' of the messianic fulfillment. . . . The teaching of Mark finds in Peter's confession not its term but its point of departure. Consequently, in the section that *follows* Peter's confession we find stronger and clearer expressions on the content of and the real motivation for the messianic secret" (*Le secret messianique*, p. 273).

26. Cf. Luke's version, which adds "daily" (9:23).

27. See Lagrange, *L'Evangile*, p. 221, for examples.

28. See J. de Guibert, *Leçons de théologie spirituelle* (Toulouse: Ed. de la Revue d'Ascétique et de Mystique, 1955), p. 119.

29. This accounts for the sometimes difficult dialogue between spiritual writers and theologians throughout the history of the church. As one example among the least suspect I may mention the trouble Ignatius Loyola had with the Inquisition and its theologians at Alcalá, Salamanca, and Paris. The difficulty for some theologians to understand new spiritual experiences finds expression, for example, in this judgment passed on Ignatius and his disciples by one of the best-known sixteenth-century theologians: "They say their manner of life is not as organized nor does it show the kind of order that is usually followed by those who are trying to excel beyond the ordinary in the religious state. . . . They do not have choir . . . or fasts or abstinences or the use of the discipline . . . nor do they wear a distinctive habit; and they adopt a presumptuous name; moreover their founder was not remarkable for miracles either in life or in death" (Melchior Cano, cited in M. Andrés, *La teología española en el siglo XVI* [Madrid: BAC, 1977], vol. 2, p. 528).

Chapter 4

1. See J. de Guibert, *Leçons de théologie spirituelle* (Toulouse: Ed. de la Revue d'Ascétique et de Mystique, 1955), pp. 9–10.

2. A discussion of Paul's texts on the subject calls for careful analysis. I therefore base my remarks on the Greek original as given in J. M. Bover and J. O'Callaghan, *Nuevo Testamento trilingüe* (Madrid: BAC, 1977), whose translation into Spanish I frequently use because of its literalness, which makes it suitable in the present context.

3. Of the 147 occurrences of *sarx* in the New Testament, 91 are in Paul. The remainder are distributed among the various other books of the New Testament; only John's use of the term (13 times) seems relevant.

4. There is a third term that is less frequently used to translate *basar:* it is *krea,* the flesh of animals that serves as food (Rom. 14:21; 1 Cor. 8:13).

5. Some interpreters regard this as the key concept in Paul: "One could say without exaggeration that the concept of body forms the keystone of Paul's theology": J. A. T. Robinson, *The Body* (Studies in Biblical Theology 5; London: SCM, 1957), p. 9.

6. Paul speaks in these texts of *pasa sarx,* "all flesh," in referring to the human person.

7. See X. Léon-Dufour, "Flesh," in X. Léon-Dufour, ed., *Dictionary of Biblical Theology* (New York: Seabury, rev. 2nd ed., 1973), p. 186: "Nowhere is flesh one of the elements in the 'composite' whole that is man. Only toward the II/III century with the beginning of rabbinic thought was anthropological dualism adopted in the Jewish world." Along the same line P. Bonnard, *L'Epître de saint Paul aux Galates* (Neuchâtel: Delachaux et Niestlé, 1972), p. 112, maintains that "there is no question here of a dualist anthropology in the sense that the human being would be (naturally) composed of two opposed principles: flesh (a lower, material, corporeal, sensual, etc., element) and spirit (a higher, luminous, divine, etc., element). The whole human person, spirit and body, is fleshy; it must renounce itself *in its entirety* if it is to obey the Spirit of God."

8. "Solidarity is not a Biblical word but it expresses better than any other word I know one of the most fundamental concepts in the Bible—the concept frequently referred to by scholars as the Hebrew notion of collectivity" (Albert Nolan, *Jesus before Christianity* [Maryknoll, N.Y.: Orbis Books, 1978], p. 59).

9. See X. Léon-Dufour, *Dictionary of the New Testament* (San Francisco: Harper & Row, 1980), pp. 197-98: "Following the thought of later Judaism in readily linking flesh and sin (without thereby making flesh out to be the source of sin), Paul stressed in his teaching a train of thought that was unknown in the O. T. Good in itself because created by God, the flesh became the source of sin in the extent to which it 'boasted before God.' "

10. Augustine pointed this out long ago: "St. Paul places animosities, quarrels, enmities, hatreds, jealousies . . . among the works of the flesh" (*De civitate Dei*, XIV, 3, 2). In the same vein, "It is clear that for Paul the flesh is not only attraction to sensuality; it can lead to acts of the intellectual order" (M. J. Lagrange, *Saint Paul. Epître au Galates* [Paris: Gabalda, 1942], p. 149).

11. An echo of this biblical perspective is found in a text by the Amerindian Guamán Poma (see chap. 1, note 5, above), written from his own eyewitness experience of the oppression suffered by indigenous peoples: "Those who did not know me but saw that I was poor made fun of me—those 'gentlemen,' their wives and daughters. They ranked me among the animals that do not have much to eat. They made me feel that I was being eaten alive—by them and by myself" (*Nueva corónica*, vol. 2, p. 913).

12. Without asserting inappropriate equivalences, I cannot but think here of José María Arguedas's anguished confession of his struggle with death: "I have struggled against death, or at least I believe I have struggled against death, very straightforwardly, by writing this broken and querulous account. My allies were few and unreliable; the allies of death won out. They are strong and were looked upon with favor by my own flesh. This account with its roughnesses reflects that unequal fight" ("¿Ultimo diario?" in *El zorro de arriba y el zorro de abajo* [Buenos Aires: Losada, 1975], p. 267).

13. Luke uses the word "spirit" in the same sense in a well-known passage: "My spirit rejoices in God my Savior" (1:47).

14. This is in keeping with the creativity of *ruah*. The story of creation says: "Then the Lord God formed man of dust from the ground, and breathed into his nostrils the breath of life; and man became a living being" (Gen. 2:7). The *ruah* is the breath of life.

15. Commentators have always pointed out the careful differentiation of the Apostle's vocabulary in this passage. He speaks of the *works* of the flesh but the *fruit* of the Spirit; see, e.g., H. Schlier, *La carta a los Gálatas* (Salamanca: Sígueme, 1975), p. 296. [German original: *Der Brief an die Galater* (Göttingen: Vandenhoeck und Ruprecht, 4th ed., 1965).] See also the recent interesting comparison of the theologies of Matthew and Paul in regard to the role of works in Christian life: D. Marguerat, *Le jugement dans l'Evangile de Matthieu* (Geneva: Labor et Fides, 1981), pp. 212-15.

16. With regard to Paul's list in the Letter to the Galatians (cited above), P. Bonnard writes: "Love in this context is chiefly fraternal love; the entire list emphasizes the social character of the new life, but it presupposes an understanding of the prior love of God. Love is mentioned first in order to show that it is the most important sign (and the only permanent one: 1 Cor. 13:8) of the Spirit in the church and that it alone gives the other virtues their Christian character" (*L'Epître*, p. 114). The same idea is found in J. M. González Ruiz, *Epístola de San Pablo a los Gálatas* (Madrid: Fax, 1971), p. 252.

17. See W. Marchel, *Abba, Père! La prière du Christ et des Chrétiens* (Analecta Biblica 19; Rome: Pontifical Biblical Institute, 1971).

18. See J. Huby, *Saint Paul: Epître aux Romains* (Paris: Beauchesne, 1957), p. 282: "In Paul 'carnal' and 'spiritual' as applied to persons do not mean that the individuals are locked into these categories so that they cannot pass from the one to the other. Grace is offered to the carnal in order that they may become spiritual, and conversely the spiritual may through deliberate negligence or cowardice fall from their state and become carnal."

19. "God is spirit," says John with clarity (John 4:24).

20. Paul's translators and interpreters point out that it is difficult to decide concretely when "spirit" ought to be written with a capital letter. But as Jacques Guillet observes, "this ambiguity, embarrassing for a translator, is a light for faith: it is the proof that the Spirit of God, while it permeates the spirit of man and transforms him, leaves man his complete personality" ("Spirit," in X. Léon-Dufour, *Dictionary of Biblical Theology* [no. 25], pp. 570-71).

21. See G. Gutiérrez, *El Dios de la vida* (Lima: Departamento de Teología de la U. C., 1982).

22. Paul uses the word "body" about 86 times, as against 30 occurrences in the gospels (in parallel passages). He uses it in particular in his more theological letters (the word does not occur at all in the so-called Pastoral Letters).

23. It is to be observed that unlike the other New Testament writers Paul never calls a corpse a "body." He uses "body" only of a living organism.

24. See R. Bultmann, *Theology of the New Testament* (New York: Scribner's, 1951), vol. 1, p. 194; cf. p. 195: "The result of all the foregoing is this: *Man, his person as a whole*, can be denoted by *soma*."

25. Robinson describes as follows the relationship between the concept of flesh and the concept of body in Paul: "While *sarx* stands for man, in the solidarity of creation, in his distance from God, *soma* stands for man, in the solidarity of creation, as made for God" (*Body*, p. 31).

26. This profound human solidarity is mirrored in the celebrated parallel between Adam and Jesus in Rom. 5:12-21.

27. See Robinson, *Body*, p. 32, n. 1.

28. See Bultmann, *Theology*, p. 201: "Thus, Paul did not dualistically distinguish between man's self (his 'soul') and his bodily *soma* as if the latter were an inappropriate shell, a prison, to the former; nor does his hope expect a release of the self from its bodily prison but expects instead the 'bodily' resurrection—or rather the transformation of the *soma* from under the power of flesh into a spiritual *soma*, i.e., a Spirit-ruled *soma*."

29. Hugo Echegaray makes this perceptive comment in his *Anunciar el Reino* (Lima: CEP, 1981), p. 45: "The biblical concept of the human being is that of a body possessing life, not that of an incarnated soul (a concept that is more in keeping with the anthropological dualism of the Greeks). But the

enlivening of this body is something that is at once biological, social, and political. It is for this reason that the spiritual includes all areas of life."

30. See Bultmann, *Theology*, p. 192: "That *soma* belongs inseparably, constitutively, to human existence is most clearly evident from the fact that Paul cannot conceive even of a future human existence after death 'when that which is perfect is come' as an existence without *soma*—in contrast with the view of those in Corinth who deny the resurrection."

31. See above, pp. 56-57.

32. As is well known, the adjective "mystical" is not found in Paul. Its first use occurs in the exegesis of the School of Alexandria; see L. Bouyer, *The Spirituality of the New Testament and the Fathers* (New York: Desclee, 1963).

33. Robinson, *Body*, p. 51, says: "It is almost impossible to exaggerate the materialism and crudity of Paul's doctrine of the church as literally now the resurrection *body* of Christ." L. Cerfaux had already written in his *The Church in the Theology of St. Paul* (New York: Herder & Herder, 1959) that the church or body of Christ "is none other than the real and personal body which lived, died, and was glorified, and with which the bread in the Eucharist is identified" (p. 278).

34. See A. Feuillet, "Le règne de la mort et le règne de la vie (Rom. 5, 12-21)," *Revue biblique*, 77 (1970): 481-521.

35. A text of the Protestant churches of Latin America says it well: "The history of salvation, to which sacred scriptures bear witness, is the history of the struggle of God together with human beings that life may triumph over the forces of death. The death of death (1 Cor. 15:26) is the final goal of the divine plan, so that life may be resplendent. 'I came,' says Jesus, 'that they may have life, and have it abundantly' (John 10:10). And by his death, he gave us life" ("Mensaje del Consejo Latinoamericano de Iglesias [CLAI] a las iglesias del continente americano," Huampaní, Peru, Nov. 1982, in *Cristianismo y sociedad*, no. 75, fasc. 1 [1983], p. 57).

36. K. Barth is of the view that the first ten verses of Romans 8 contain the language precisely of a "decision"; see his *The Epistle to the Romans* (London: Oxford University Press, 1933), p. 271.

37. P. Lamarche and C. Le Dû rightly observe: "Christian activity is not a prior condition of salvation, but a consequence of it. And the freedom of the Spirit guides the Christians to help them discern and find their way to God in love. This Pauline doctrine seems very simple, but logical, literary, and intellectual prejudgments have often obscured the text" (*Epître aux Romains V-VIII. Structure littéraire et sens* [Paris: Editions du CNRS, 1980], p. 82).

38. See P. Richard, "Espiritualidad para tiempo de revolución. Teología espiritual a la luz de San Pablo," in E. Bonnín, ed., *Espiritualidad y libera-*

ción en América Latina (San José, Costa Rica: DEI, n.d. [1982]), p. 96: "The transformation of the body under the action of the Spirit; the conquest of death by the resurrection; and the anticipation of all this through faith and hope: these add up to the only spirituality that enables us to seek and find the living God of Jesus Christ."

39. According to Luke, when the risen Jesus appears to his disciples he says to them: " 'See my hands and my feet, that it is I myself; handle me, and see; for a spirit has not flesh and bones [*sarka kai ostea*] as you see that I have.' And when he had said this he showed them his hands and his feet. And while they still disbelieved for joy, and wondered, he said to them, 'Have you anything here to eat?' They gave him a piece of broiled fish, and he took it and ate it before them" (24:39–43).

Chapter 5

1. With regard to the Jewish people's experience—social and communal as well as individual and interior—of God's mercy, John Paul II writes in his encyclical *Rich in Mercy*, no. 4: "Behind the many-faceted conviction of this community and the individuals in it, a conviction shown by the entire Old Testament through the centuries, lies the *early experience* of the chosen people at the time of the exodus when the Lord saw the wretched state of his enslaved people and, hearing their cry and seeing their affliction, determined to set them free. In this saving act of the Lord the prophet could see both [God's] love and . . . compassion at work. This, then, is the basis for the security of the people as a whole and each of its members: the divine mercy upon which human beings can call in every adversity" (*The Pope Speaks*, 26 [1981]: 27, italics added).

2. At the conclusion of an exhaustive linguistic and theological study of the oppression of the people of the Old Testament, Jacques Pons writes: "The spectacle of the world opens our eyes and sharpens the mind of the exegete to penetrate to the depth of the Old Testament, study all its words in isolation, and then bring them together for mutual illumination. A ray of biblical light can then illuminate the world in which we live, in order to scatter the forces of oppression from their hiding places and expose them for what they are: not something inadvertently off-course, not an accident of history, but the irruption of death and chaos in God's creation" (*L'oppression dans l'Ancien Testament* [Paris: Letouzey et Ané, 1981], p. 211). On the theme of oppression in the Bible, see also Elsa Tamez, *Bible of the Oppressed* (Maryknoll, N.Y.: Orbis, 1982).

3. See A. Neher, *Moses and the Vocation of the Jewish People* (New York: Harper Torchbooks, 1959), pp. 136–37: "The first thing that is expressed in the Jewish Passover is the certainty of freedom. With the exodus a

new age has struck for humanity: redemption from misery. . . . All constraint is accidental; all misery is only provisional. The breath of freedom which has blown over the world since the exodus can dispel them this very day.''

4. With respect to God's revelation in the exodus, Juan Alfaro brings out the rich and full relationship between the Old and New Testaments: ''The writings of the New Testament see in the death and resurrection of Christ the definitive fulfillment of the promises of the covenant, the definitive passover, our liberation from sin and death. We Christians can thus fall into the error of reducing the entire significance of the exodus to a mere anticipatory promise of the redemption of humankind by Christ. To be sure, the ultimate meaning of Yahweh's covenant with Israel is the liberation accomplished in Christ. But the event of the exodus has also its own meaning: Yahweh's self-revelation in the liberation of an oppressed people. Liberation from oppression is seen as a revelatory act of God—indeed as the act of God that inaugurates the history of salvation.''

5. The concrete form that the occupation of Canaan took is debated by scholars. See the controversial but very interesting and heavily documented work of N. K. Gottwald, *The Tribes of Yahweh: A Sociology of the Religion of Liberated Israel, 1250–1050 B.C.* (Maryknoll, N.Y.: Orbis, 1979).

6. In a pastoral letter published on the occasion of the twenty-fifth anniversary of his episcopal consecration, Bishop Luis Vallejos reminded the rural poor of his diocese of this great biblical concept: ''I want to inspire hope in you. To tell you you should love the land with its fruits—your seed, your animals, your tools. . . . I want to tell you you should love your culture, your songs, your language, your way of doing things, your family, your landscape. That along with the other poor you should make preparations and organize, because in unity alone is there strength. That sooner or later you or your children will possess the entire land because God has given it to all as a gift and a task. God is the sole true owner of the fields'' (in *Dos obispos del Sur Andino* [Lima: CEP, 1982], p. 68).

7. See the *Traduction oecuménique de la Bible* (Paris: Cerf, 1975), p. 384, note on Acts 9:2: '' 'Way' would normally mean a manner of life and action—conduct. But to this abstract meaning Acts, and Acts alone, adds a new meaning: the term is one of those used to signify 'Christians' as followers of *the way of the Lord, of God*, which is the way of salvation.''

8. They argue from the fact that in Acts 16:17 (''they proclaim a way of salvation'') and 18:25–26 (''he had been given instruction in the way of the Lord'') there is an allusion to the message of Jesus; they also connect 13:10 (''the straight paths of the Lord'') with 13:12 (''the teaching of the Lord'').

9. Commenting on various interpretations of the idea of ''way'' in Acts, S. Lyonnet writes: ''A first and obvious conclusion is inescapable: the Christian religion was conceived as essentially a form of ethical behavior; this evidently supposes an attitude of mind, but it is at the same time a manner of

acting'' (''La 'Voie' dans les Actes des Apôtres,'' in J. Delorme and J. Duplacy, eds., *La Parole de grâce. Etudes lucaniennes à la mémoire d'Augustin George* [Paris: Recherches de Science Religieuse, 1981], pp. 152–53).

10. See A. Gelin, *The Key Concepts of the Old Testament* (New York: Sheed & Ward, 1955), pp. 82–83: ''This term [*derek*, 'way'] is typical of the Hebrew genius: whereas in Hellenism the same metaphor (*methodos*) applies to an intellectual process, in the Bible it refers to moral behavior.''

11. See J. Dupont, *Etudes sur les Actes des Apôtres* (Paris: Cerf, 1967), p. 475: ''To define the way is to define Christian morality—that is, the manner in which Christians try to serve God in all that they do.''

12. In ''Liberté chrétienne et loi de l'Esprit,'' *Christus*, 4 (1954): 12, S. Lyonnet explains why Paul speaks of the ''law'' of the Spirit: ''If the Apostle uses 'law' to describe this spiritual dynamism instead of using the word 'grace' as he does in other passages (Rom. 6:4), it is surely because he is referring to Jeremiah's prophecy . . . of the new covenant, the 'New Testament'; there the prophet, too, spoke of a 'law': 'I will put my law in their hearts' (Jer. 31:33).''

13. This is in accordance with the words of Jesus himself: ''I am the way, and the truth, and the life'' (John 14:6). John Paul II in his encyclical *Redeemer of the Human Race*, no. 13, says: ''Jesus Christ is the principal way for the church. He is also our way 'to the Father' (John 14:1ff.) and to every individual human being. No one has a right to hold the church back on this way that leads from Christ to the person, on this way by which Christ is linked to individual human beings. The temporal good of human beings and their eternal good as well require this activity of the church'' (*The Pope Speaks*, 24 [1979]: 116).

14. ''Jesus taught the way of God with freedom; this provoked opposition. He is reproached for doing things that make others think he is a sinner. . . . That he is not, that he takes up a prophetic role and lives with a freedom that no one truly fearful of God can take from him, shakes the social and religious equilibrium of the Judaism of the first century. The authority and freedom of Jesus explain the conflicts that his preaching provoked. They will eventually lead to his condemnation'' (C. Duquoc, *Jésus, homme libre* [Paris: Cerf, 1974], pp. 38–39).

15. S. Lyonnet sums up as follows his own interpretation of Christian freedom in St. Paul: ''The Christians who are moved by the Spirit, and to the extent that they are so moved, are liberated in Christ not only from the Mosaic law as Mosaic but from the Mosaic law as law; in other words, they are freed of every law that coerces (I do not say 'obliges') the person from without, but they do not on that account become amoral beings located beyond good and evil'' (''Liberté,'' p. 2).

16. See the biblical reflection on the ''Galilean journey'' of the Mexican-American people in the excellent work by Virgilio Elizondo, *Galilean Jour-*

ney: The Mexican-American Promise (Maryknoll, N.Y.: Orbis, 1983).

17. *Ascent of Mount Carmel*, I, 2, 1, in *The Collected Works of St. John of the Cross* (Garden City, N.Y.: Doubleday, 1964; paperback reprint: Washington, D.C.: Institute of Carmelite Studies, 1973), p. 75 [henceforth: Kavanaugh, with page number]. John of the Cross says of this process, the "journey of the soul toward union with God is called a night" (Kavanaugh 74).

18. *Ascent*, I, 1, 1 (Kavanaugh 73).

19. *The Dark Night*, II, 12, title (Kavanaugh 355).

20. *Ascent*, I, 2, 1 (Kavanaugh 74).

21. *Ascent*, I, 1 (Kavanaugh 73).

22. *Ascent*, I, 1, 1 and 4 (Kavanaugh 73–74).

23. Ibid.

24. *Ascent*, I, 15, 2 (Kavanaugh 106).

25. *Ascent*, I, 2, 1 (Kavanaugh 74).

26. *Ascent*, II, 1, Stanza, and 2 (Kavanaugh 107–8).

27. *Ascent*, II, 2, 2 (Kavanaugh 109).

28. *Ascent*, I, 11, 5 (Kavanaugh 97).

29. *Spiritual Canticle*, Stanza 35 (Kavanaugh 414). The idea of life according to the Spirit as a "way" is a classic one in the history of spirituality. Ignatius of Loyola liked to sign his letters "The poor pilgrim"; he describes himself in the same way in his autobiographical notes.

30. *The Dark Night*, II, 17, 6 (Kavanaugh 370).

31. *The Dark Night*, II, 17, 8 (Kavanaugh 370).

32. Kavanaugh 67.

33. St. Ignatius of Loyola, *The Constitutions of the Society of Jesus* (St. Louis: Institute of Jesuit Sources, 1970), p. 119.

34. St. John of the Cross, *Ascent*, I, 11, 6 (Kavanaugh 98).

35. *Ascent*, I, 2, 1 (Kavanaugh 75).

36. *Ascent*, II, 2, 1 (Kavanaugh 109).

37. *Ascent*, Stanza 8 (Kavanaugh 69). Luis Espinal aspires to this same condition on the basis of his experience of solidarity with the poor of Bolivia:

> Lord of the night and the void,
> we yearned to sink softly
> into your impalpable lap,
> trustingly,
> with the security children feel.

("Crisis," in *Oraciones a Quemarropa* [Lima: CEP, 1982], p. 82).

38. See *A Theology of Liberation*, p. 203: "Theological categories are not enough. We need a vital attitude, all-embracing and synthesizing, informing the totality as well as every detail of our lives; we need a 'spirituality.' "

39. *The Way of Perfection* (El Escorial text), 48, 4.

40. I indicated something of this earlier (chap. 3) when I pointed out a relationship between spiritualities and historical movements.

41. See *A Theology of Liberation*, p. 204: "Not only is there a contemporary history and a contemporary gospel; there is also a contemporary spiritual experience which cannot be overlooked. A spirituality means a reordering of the great axes of the Christian life in terms of this contemporary experience. What is new is the synthesis this reordering brings about, in stimulating a deepened understanding of various ideas, in bringing to the surface unknown or forgotten aspects of the Christian life, and, above all, in the way in which these things are converted into life, prayer, commitment, and action." Thus J. B. Metz writes: "It is necessary that the one and only discipleship have many disciples, that the one and only witness have many witnesses, that the one and only hope have many who hope" (*Un credo per l'uomo d'oggi* [Brescia: Queriniana, 1976], p. 49).

42. J. de Guibert points out that "if we ask what the source is of the variety of spiritual formulas that we see in the church," the answer must be that "at the point of departure there is always an original experience . . . one that gives birth to a new school of spirituality" (*Leçons de théologie spirituelle* [Toulouse: Ed. de la Revue d'Ascétique et de Mystique: 1955], p. 171). Nonetheless he makes little or no reference in his book to the broad historical contexts of these experiences.

43. This is expressed well in a prayer of a Peruvian university community: "We want to consecrate to you our imperfect pilgrimage, the course of our faith and our pledge—since our first call, since the coming together of this beloved community, since our agreement to our commitment. If we have faith nowadays, Lord, it is because we have experienced you in our weak but growing experience of identification with the people" ("Prayer for Easter Sunday," in SL, p. 300).

Part Three

1. In *Octogesima Adveniens*, no. 47, Paul VI wrote: "It is by losing himself in God who sets him free that man finds true freedom, renewed in the death and resurrection of the Lord" (in J. Gremillion, *The Gospel of Peace and Justice: Catholic Social Teaching since Pope John* [Maryknoll, N.Y.: Orbis, 1976], p. 509). Along the same lines Dietrich Bonhoeffer wrote: "In the language of the Bible freedom is not something man has for himself but something he has for others. . . . It is not a possession, a presence, an object . . . but a relationship and nothing else. In truth, freedom is a relationship between two persons. Being free means 'being free for the other,' because the other has bound me to him. Only in relationship with the other am I free" (*Creation and Fall/Temptation* [New York: Macmillan, 1959], p. 37).

2. This is a fundamental insight in the theology of liberation; see *A Theology of Liberation*, pp. 35-36.

3. See my *El Dios de la vida* (Lima: Departamento de Teología de la U.C., 1982), pp. 18-19.

4. Ignatian spirituality is a clear example of the connection between freedom and love. "Election" is doubtless a key moment in the *Spiritual Exercises*, but I think that it takes on its full meaning only in the "contemplation for obtaining love." It is in love that a free election finds its full meaning. "Free to love" proves to be a formula equivalent to the one that has traditionally been taken as characterizing the spirituality of Ignatius—namely, "contemplative in action." On some significant aspects of Ignatian spirituality, see R. Antoncich, *Ejercicios y liberación del hombre* (Lima: Centro Ignaciano de Espiritualidad, 1983).

5. See J. Riera, "¿Crisis de espiritualidad o algo nuevo que está naciendo?" in *Acompañando a la comunidad* (Lima: CEP, 1982), pp. 38-69; Jorge Alvarez Calderón, "Descubrir la espiritualidad del pueblo," ibid., pp. 169-80.

6. In connection with the reading of some passages of the Bible, John Paul II said during his visit to Brazil that "since its beginning the church has continually meditated on these passages and messages, but it is aware that it has not yet plumbed their depths as it would like (will it perhaps do so some day?). In varying concrete situations it *rereads these texts* and scrutinizes the message they contain, in the desire of discovering *a new application* for them" (homily at Salvador [Bahia], July 7, 1980, in *Pronunciamentos do Papa no Brasil* [São Paulo: Loyola, 1980], p. 192; italics added).

Chapter 6

1. See *A Theology of Liberation*, p. 205: "Evangelical conversion is indeed the touchstone of all spirituality. Conversion means a radical transformation of ourselves; it means thinking, feeling, and living as Christ—present in exploited and alienated man."

2. R. Schnackenburg, *Christian Existence in the New Testament* (University of Notre Dame Press, 1968), vol. 1, p. 36: "We turn back from the wrong direction and take a new route."

3. Pastoral ministers, priests, religious women, and pastors of Bolivia, Jan. 20, 1973, in *Praxis del martirio ayer y hoy* (Bogotá: CEPLA, 1977), pp. 125-26. Or again: "In view of the fact that we ought to be engaged in struggle and in view of the suffering of our people, individualism, fearfulness, and cowardice are sins" (from the Fourth Meeting of the Christians of Puno [Peru], 1980; text published in RIMAC, the documentation service of the Instituto Bartolomé de Las Casas).

4. One example: "The luxury of a few becomes an insult to the wretched

poverty of the vast masses. This is contrary to the plan of the Creator and to the honor that is due him. In this anxiety and sorrow the church sees a situation of social sinfulness, all the more serious because it exists in countries that call themselves Catholic and are capable of changing the situation'' (PD, no. 28).

5. ''She [the Virgin Mary] makes it possible for us to overcome the manifold 'structures of sin' in which our lives—personal, familial, and social—are encased. She makes it possible for us to obtain the grace of true liberation— the liberation by which Christ has liberated humankind in its entirety'' (homily in the Shrine of Our Lady of Zapopan, no. 3).

6. ''Evangelización: Algunas lineas pastorales,'' in *Documentos del episcopado: La Pastoral conciliar en el Perú, en la Iglesia 1968-1977* (Lima, Ed. Apostolado de la Prensa), p. 185.

7. Pastoral exhortation in *Boletín del arzobispado* (Oct. 1978), p. 36.

8. Homily on Feb. 16, 1979. In the same perspective the Episcopal Conference of El Salvador wrote in its message of March 5, 1977: ''This is the fundamental sin that we pastors must denounce. There can be no ignoring of the people or playing with it and its hopes. As long as no determined and effective effort is made to solve the problems of the distribution of wealth and land, of participation in government, and of the organization of rural and urban inhabitants, their status as citizens and children of God is being ignored'' (in SLE, p. 275a).

9. ''It has been said that interior conversion does not suffice, that we are held to perfect and progressively reconquer our entire being for God. Today we must be aware that what we must reconquer and reform is our entire world. In other words, personal conversion and structural reform cannot be separated'' (Pedro Arrupe, in *Vie chrétienne*, 178 [June 1975]).

10. Address at Louvain University (Feb. 2, 1980), in SVF, p. 372a.

11. ''Declaración'' (Sept. 5, 1977), in SLE, p. 57a.

12. ''Unidos en la esperanza'' (July 25, 1976), in SLE, p. 86a. Here is another and similar passage: ''It cannot be denied that the church and Christians are passing through a painful but real process of conversion. Since Vatican II and more particularly since Medellín, they have been becoming more aware of the radical no that God says to our sins of omission. In a greater or lesser degree we have set about collaborating for a more human society that, as we Christians see it, means the approach of the reign of God'' (Episcopal Conference of El Salvador, March 5, 1977, in SLE, p. 181b).

13. Vicaría de la Solidaridad de Santiago, Chile, ''Abrir la huella del Buen Samaritano'' (1976), in SLE, p. 140a.

14. See the encyclical *On Human Work* in which the church is called to solidarity with the just claims of worker movements (no. 8).

15. See G. Thils, *Théologie des réalités terrestres* (Bruges: Desclée de Brouwer, 1946), vol. 1.

16. This is in agreement with Berdyaev's statement: "If I am hungry, that is a material problem; if someone else is hungry, that is a spiritual problem."

17. R. Grande, a Jesuit priest murdered in El Salvador, homily at Apopa (Feb. 13, 1977), in SLE, p. 260a. See Martin Lange and Reinhold Iblacker, eds., *Witnesses of Hope* (Maryknoll, N.Y.: Orbis, 1981), pp. 27–33.

18. "Cuaresma y conversión" (March 10, 1972), in SLE, p. 272a.

19. Pope John Paul II, writing on the spirituality of work, says: "The entire human person, body and spirit, participates in work, whether it be manual or intellectual. And the word of the living God, the gospel of salvation, is addressed not to a part of the human being, but the entirety" (*On Human Work*, no. 24).

20. In *Nicaragua a un año de la victoria* (Lima: CEP, 1980), p. 72.

21. Since the sixteenth century the situation of poverty and oppression of the Amerindians has turned their defenders to this gospel text. And it inspired the celebrated expression of Bartolomé de Las Casas—the "flogged Christs of the Indies." The Amerindian, Guamán Poma, has said, with deep biblical rootage: "It seems to the rich and haughty that where a poor person is, God and justice are not. But it must be understood in the faith that where a poor person is, there is Jesus Christ; and where God is, there is justice" (*Nueva corónica*, vol. 2, p. 903).

22. Where such bonds exist, the lowly open their world to all those who are in solidarity with them. At the burial of Fr. Vicente Hondarza (of Huacho, Peru), who died under circumstances that have never been explained, a *campesino* said: "For us field-workers it is hard to express what the physical absence of Fr. Vicente means. He was a priest who understood the meaning of the church; a priest who shared his life working with the neediest, always bringing the gospel message to the poor, to those in need, to workers in the fields. We are saddened because we have lost a beloved companion" (in *Páginas*, 54 [1983] 31). In a similar vein Bishop Martín Zegarra, the bishop of Santiago de Veraguas, Panama, wrote after the disappearance of Fr. Héctor Gallego: "I assure you, Héctor, that we think about you, that we love you, that we admire what you did for the poor, the needy, those who are the object of God's predilection, of our Father who is the Truth and who wants us to search the truth in full and live an authentic freedom. Do you know what, Héctor? I cannot believe that you will not return" (1971, in SL, p. 68).

23. St. John of the Cross, *Ascent of Mount Carmel*, I, 4, 3 (Kavanaugh 78).

24. As Paul did and his letters show: "God is my witness, how I yearn for you all with the affection of Christ Jesus" (Phil. 1:8).

25. A group of Chilean Christians, Nov. 1973, in SLE, p. 9b.

26. Bishop Enrique Alvear, "La toma en Pudahuel y el drama de las familias sin casa" (1981), in SVF, p. 188b.

27. Statement of the Conference of Religious of Guatemala regarding the problems of El Quiché (Aug. 1980), in SVF, p. 441b.

28. Homily of Jan. 21, 1979.

29. *Way of Perfection* (New York: Sheed & Ward, 1946; Image Books, 1964), p. 150. For a brief presentation of the witness of Teresa of Avila, see María del Carmen Diez, "Teresa de Avila doctora de la experiencia," in *Páginas*, 40 (Sept. 1981) 10–14. In language free of cliché a Christian *campesino* remarked at a gathering: "I believe that the reign of God exists right in the harsh life of the people, because there are many weaknesses, aren't there? Sometimes a man gets weary, but something gives him a push. Then it is in the very strength of the people that the reign of God is to be found" (fourth meeting of the Christians of Puno, 1980). "Something gives him a push" and keeps him from drawing back.

Chapter 7

1. Address at Louvain University (Feb. 2, 1980), in SVF, p. 372b.

2. CLAR, *Documento de la IV Asamblea General* (Dec. 1969), in SL, p. 279a.

3. In J. de Guibert, *The Jesuits, Their Spiritual Doctrine and Practice: A Historical Study* (Chicago: Institute of Jesuit Sources, 1964), p. 148, n. 55. There are several versions of this Ignatian maxim. I have cited the one that goes back to Pedro Ribadaneira and is to be found in the *Monumenta Ignatiana*. For a penetrating, though at times somewhat forced, study of this and similar formulations, see G. Fessard, *La dialectique des Exercices spirituels de Saint Ignace de Loyola* (Paris: Aubier, 1956), vol. 1, pp. 303–63.

4. See L. Cerfaux, *L'itinéraire spirituel de saint Paul* (Paris: Cerf. 1966), pp. 132–35. For the ecclesiological implications of *koinonia*, see M. Legido López, *Fraternidad en el mundo* (Salamanca: Sígueme, 1982), esp. pp. 209–86.

5. See *A Theology of Liberation*, pp. 205–6: "A spirituality of liberation must be filled with a living sense of *gratuitousness*. Communion with the Lord and with all men is more than anything else a gift. . . . The knowledge that at the root of our personal and community existence lies the gift of the self-communication with God, the grace of his friendship, fills our life with gratitude."

6. See H. Echegaray, "Conocer a Dios es practicar la justicia," in *Anunciar el Reino* (Lima: CEP, 1981): "The measure of our fidelity depends not on the native capacities of our own hearts but on the abundant gifts that the Lord bestows on us. The word of God awakens profound and unforeseeable energies."

7. This is the insight possessed by many who are committed to this struggle. Juan Gonzalo Rose, in exile for political reasons, has said it beautifully in a poem to his sister (*Carta a María Teresa*):

> I ask myself now
> why I do not limit my love
> to the sudden roses,
> the tides of June,
> the moons over the sea?
> Why have I had to love
> the rose *and* justice,
> the sea *and* justice,
> justice *and* the light?

The same testimony is given by the lowly but heroic people of Nicaragua, a people of poets who are able to combine constancy in defending their right to life and dignity with the cultivation of beauty in song and poetry.

8. In her *Life*, chap. 8.

9. See the interesting anthology of prayers composed in Latin America compiled by Charles Antoine, *L'Amérique latine en priére* (Paris: Cerf, 1981).

10. On this point, see Juan Hernández Pico, "La oración en los procesos latinoamericanos de liberación," in A. Cussiánovich et al., *Espiritualidad de la liberación* (Lima: CEP, 1980), pp. 159-85; and Frei Betto, "Oração, exigencia (tambem) política," *Revista Eclesiástica Brasileira*, 42 (1982) 444-55.

11. Henri Nouwen, after a stay in Bolivia and Peru, has written that there he learned how to say *gracias*, "thanks." The familiar expression *demos gracias* ("let us give thanks") became for him something more than a prayer said before eating: he now understands it in the sense of projecting the whole of life in the presence of God and all God's people in an atmosphere of gratitude (*Gracias: A Latin American Journal* [San Francisco: Harper & Row, 1983], p. 187).

12. I offer as an example the following prayer in which Bishop José Dammert sums up the feelings of his people: "Lord, the men and women of the Andes cry to you because of the utter poverty in which we live, subject to the vagaries of nature and even more to oppression by other human beings. With resignation and patience and while contemplating the sorrowful passion of your Son as an image of our own sufferings, we have for centuries endured the scarcity of food and the lack of work for a large majority of our young who have no alternatives but wretchedness and delinquency. There is no future for them on a tiny parcel of land that is exhausted by millennia of tilling. The fruit of our labor in fields and mines is appropriated by others who leave us but a few crumbs. Necessity compels us men and women of the Andes to toil from childhood on, and the harshness of our life leaves us no respite.

"We know, nonetheless, that you are a God of mercy and that you take pity on the needy. Therefore we renew our cries—often in silence like Mary at the foot of the cross—from the depths of our hearts. We adore your providence and we intensify our hope of the human fellowship that your Christ teaches us and that we practice with generous hospitality" (*Veinticinco años al servicio de la Iglesia* [Lima: CEP, 1983], pp. 248–49).

13. Letter from the communities of El Quiché, Jan. 1981, after the massacre in that part of Guatemala and the forced withdrawal of the bishop and pastoral ministers, in *Morir y despertar en Guatemala* (Lima: CEP, 1981), p. 144. The same attitude finds expression in this prayer of Luis Espinal, a Jesuit priest murdered in Bolivia: "Lord of mystery, let us feel your presence at the heart of life; we desire to find you in the depths of everyday things" (*Oraciones a Quemarropa*, p. 32).

14. *A Theology of Liberation*, pp. 206–7.

15. This is why some have now been paraphrasing the well-known "contemplative in action" of Ignatian spirituality and speaking of "contemplatives in political action," in action that changes history. See G. Gutiérrez, "Praxis de liberación y fe cristiana," in SL, p. 24; L. Boff, "Contemplativus in liberatione," in Cussiánovich, *Espiritualidad*, p. 119.

Chapter 8

1. For example, this simple testimony from a woman of the people and mother of two murdered catechists: "This is a very painful incident for us. But my sons did not die; they live on in the hearts of the people, and their blood gives life to the community; they have carried out the will of God. All those who give their lives for the sake of the others and who lead a Christian life as did my dear ones, and my dear companions, and my dear brother, are doing God's will" (Letter from Mrs. Erlinda, of Barrancabermeja, Colombia, in SVF, pp. 489–90). The Latin American masses sing of this life and this hope; see Gilmer Torres, *La sangre de los mártires* (Lima: CEP, 1981).

2. As John Paul II said on the first anniversary of the death of Oscar Romero: "A year has passed since the tragic death of Archbishop Romero, a zealous pastor who was murdered on March 24, 1980, while celebrating Mass. He thus crowned with his blood a ministry that was especially solicitous of the poorest and most marginalized. His death was a witness that has remained as the symbol of the torment of a people but also as a reason for hope of a better future" (*L'Osservatore romano*, March 29, 1981, p. 4).

3. "Cruz y resurrección," a pastoral exhortation of Feb. 26, 1978, in *Boletín del arzobispado de Lima* (Aug. 1978), p. 4.

4. Faced with serious incidents of "indiscriminate repression," the subjection of "students and rural poor to the practice of torture," and the "imprisonment of priests, seminarians, and institutional personnel of the church," the bishops of Paraguay stated in 1976: "We demand that, in view of the supreme laws of this country and the number of the baptized, an end be put to *the defamation campaign being waged against the church*. Under the

pretext of defending it, government officials and agencies have been carrying on this campaign against bishops, priests, active lay persons, and church organizations. In the de facto circumstances, what we are experiencing is *true and undisguised persecution of the church*" ("Persecucion a la Iglesia en Paraguay," RIMAC, documentation service of the Instituto Bartolomé de Las Casas, June 12, 1976). The use of the term "persecution" is certainly justified here, and—despite the refusal of some to acknowledge it—elsewhere in Latin America.

5. Comunicado de la Conferencia Episcopal de Guatemala (Aug. 6, 1981), in *Morir y despertar en Guatemala* (Lima: CEP, 1981), p. 118. Similarly: "The suffering of so many sisters and brothers is united to the torrent of Christ's blood. It is a torrent that motivates all our efforts for a geniune reconciliation" (Bishop Luis Bambaren, address at the III Congreso de la Federación de Familiares de Detenidos-Desaparecidos de América Latina, Nov. 1982, in *Páginas* [Nov.-Dec. 1982] 38). See the impressive testimony communicated by Pilar Coll in *Acompañando a la comunidad* (Lima: CEP, 1982), pp. 235-54.

6. Karl Rahner has argued for a widening of the traditional concept of martyrdom, which he describes as "the fact of accepting death for the faith in a free and resigned attitude, not actively struggling in the manner of soldiers." After examining the contemporary situation and noting that "the death of Jesus, 'passively accepted,' was the consequence of his struggle against those who wielded religious and political power at that time," the German theologian asserts that "in any case, the differences between death for the sake of the faith in an active struggle and death for the sake of the faith passively sustained are too fluid and difficult to be precise, so that the two forms of death could be conceptually distinguished and not be given the same designation. In both cases acceptance is the same and death results from the same Christian conviction. In both cases death is the acceptance of the death of Christ": "Dimensiones del martirio," *Concilium*, 183 (March 1983), 321-24. This entire issue of *Concilium* is dedicated to the theme of martyrdom, with important contributions by Leonardo Boff, Pedro Casaldáliga, J. Hernández Pico, and the South African bishop, Desmond Tutu.

7. Bishop Luis María Estrada, "Carta a las comunidades cristianas de Izabal" (July 23, 1981), in *Morir y despertar*, p. 157. Shortly after the murder of Rutilio Grande, Christian communities in Guatemala wrote that his testimony impelled them to work for the kingdom of God: "The witness of Fr. Rutilio Grande and other martyrs of Central America motivates us to work for the kingdom—that is, for a future in which there is no death, hunger, illness, a future of fellowship; it motivates us to live our faith, our hope, and our love with greater depth and effectiveness, as well as to strengthen and intensify our union with the entire Christian people of Central America" (SLE, p. 262a). The assurance that the blood of so many simple persons is the

seed of life is repeated by Archbishop Romero: "I am sure that so much bloodshed and so much suffering caused to the families of so many victims will not have been shed in vain. This blood and this suffering will fertilize a new and increasingly extensive seed, producing Salvadorans who will be conscious of their responsibility to build a more just and human society. This blood and this suffering will bear fruit in the bold, radical structural reforms that our country so urgently needs" (homily of Jan. 27, 1980).

8. As Christians we cannot, in fact, desire that there be executioners. Georges Bernanos, in his *Dialogue des Carmelites*, a work that treats with profundity and beauty the question of martyrdom and that of spiritual childhood (one of the great themes of the author), has the elderly prioress say to some nuns who want to be martyrs, "You pray for sinners, for their conversion, their repentance. How can you, at the same time, desire that they murder consecrated persons? Let us speak frankly: a Carmelite who desires martyrdom is as bad a Carmelite as a soldier would be who kills before he has orders from his superiors" (Paris: Seuil, 1949, p. 111). It is not Mother Marie, who wants the honor of martyrdom, who is guillotined, but the timid Sister Blanche, though her fear never dissipated. As the prioress says, "What God wants to test in you is not strength but weakness" (ibid., p. 34).

9. "No queremos mártires" (unfinished rough draft found on his desk), in *Oraciones a Quemarropa* (Lima: CEP, 1982), p. 12.

10. Letter dated Jan. 1981, in SVF, p. 443a; italics added.

11. *Anunciar el Reino* (Lima: CEP, 1981), p. 97.

12. Letter of Bishop Pedro Casaldáliga (Oct. 19, 1976), in SLE, pp. 254–55.

13. Against the background of the Nicaraguan experience a group of Christians writes: "And we invite all our brothers and sisters, all of our people, to enkindle throughout Nicaragua new fires of comradely love and support. We invite them to assist us by sharing our work, our food, and our song, and by recovering even the laughter and good humor that aid us in advancing through this hard and lengthy predawn until the full appearance of the new day, and that do not allow fatigue to hold us back, because behind us are coming fellow peoples still journeying in their night. Christ in his Passover is our sun, and in him Oscar Arnulfo Romero and all our sacrificed brothers and sisters shed their light on us" ("Fidelidad cristiana en el proceso de Nicaragua" [March 24, 1981], in *Nicaragua: La hora de los desafíos* [Lima: CEP, 1981], p. 147).

14. Bishops and missionaries of Brazil, "El indio, aquel que debe morir" (Dec. 25, 1973), in SLE, p. 98a.

15. "I do not doubt your interior strength. You know that you have with you the living presence of Christ who will not fail you. The followers of the 'flesh' cannot understand this. Be *witnesses* to what does not die and is not slain by weapons or by the fruits of sin and their consequences. I share your

suffering and joy as I do that of so many others. Those who believe must be *witnesses to the paschal mystery*" (Bishop Enrique Angelelli, "Carta a dos sacerdotes detenidos" [Feb. 27, 1972], in SL, p. 281a).

16. Letter of Aug. 8, 1975 (Argentina), in *Praxis de martirio ayer y hoy* (Bogotá: CEPLA, 1977), p. 29. In the same perspective: "The resurrection of the Lord, which demonstrates his sovereign power, is incompatible with an attitude of discouragement or faintheartedness, because the resurrection is proof of the divine logic that in order to establish the kingdom uses for its weapons the strength of the weak and the wisdom of the simple" (bishops and missionaries of Brazil, "El indio," in SLE, p. 98a).

17. See Bishop Estrada, letter cited in n. 5, above: "Although we often feel weak and are assailed by anxious fear of what may happen to us humanly, we know that the Lord will not let us slip from his merciful hand and that at the opportune moment we can count on his peace and on the strength that comes only from God" (p. 155).

18. A group of Peruvian bishops made the following courageous and humble statement: "We intend solidarity with the movement of the oppressed, and this in deeds and not in words alone. An expression of this intention may be seen in the way the church is trying to direct its pastoral ministry and its pronouncements in times of difficulty for the people. Because of this our church of the Sur-Andino, despite all its limitations, has awakened the distrust of the groups that exercise power" (Bishops of the Sur-Andino, "Acompañando a nuestro pueblo" [Sept. 1978], in SVF, p. 265b).

19. This is a source of joy to those who work alongside the people: "We shall joyfully share in undertakings and shall bless all the works that the people regards as its own and that are a positive step toward their liberation" (letter of Bishop Luis Dalle and twenty-six pastoral ministers in the prelature of Ayaviri, in *Dos obispos del Sur-Andino: Luis Vallejos, Luis Dalle, en el corazón de su pueblo* [Lima: CEP, 1982], p. 131).

20. "Carta a los católicos de Chile" (Dec. 17, 1982), in SVF, p. 243b.

21. National Conference of the Religious of Nicaragua, "Mensaje" (Aug. 19, 1979), in *Nicaragua a un año de la victoria* (Lima: CEP, 1980), p. 59.

22. "Oración de mi sacerdocio," written in Rome in 1974 on the occasion of the twenty-fifth anniversary of his priestly ordination, in SLE, p. 251b.

Chapter 9

1. "Pobreza y vida religiosa en América Latina" (Bogotá, 1970), p. 53; cf. Medellín, "Poverty," no. 16.

2. Statement of Aug. 6, 1981, in *Morir y despertar en Guatemala* (Lima: CEP, 1981), p. 117.

3. *En torno al documento de evangelización. Algunas líneas pastorales de la Conferencia Episcopal* (Lima: Editorial Salesiana, 1973), p. 30.

4. "An indispensable condition for the credibility of the church is its incarnation in the world of the poor" (Jon Sobrino, "La esperanza de los pobres en América Latina," *Diakonia*, 25 [March 1983]: 18); see also A. Cussiánovich, "Espiritualidad cristiana y liberadora. Continuidad y novedad," in *Espiritualidad de la liberación* (Lima: CEP, 1980), pp. 35–50.

5. We meet significant examples of this in the history of spirituality. St. Dominic decided to sell his possessions and books, saying: "I will not study on dead skins while men are dying of hunger" (cited in M.-H. Vicaire, *Saint Dominic and His Times* [New York: McGraw-Hill, 1964], p. 30).

6. *Luis Espinal: El grito de un pueblo* (Lima: CEP, 1981), p. 44.

7. Jorge Alvarez Calderón says with good reason: "I must make mention of our Latin American martyrs. They are the supreme expression of a spirituality that is lived out to its ultimate consequences. It is impossible to understand them [these individuals] except within this process of painful awakening and in direct or indirect connection with organizations of the people. The majority of them are anonymous—because the situation in our countries is such that it is still not possible to know the lowly by their names—but nonetheless when they are called they set no limits to their human love. They live out the words of Christ in a concrete way: 'No one takes my life from me; I myself give it' (John 10:18)" ("Descubrir la espiritualidad del pueblo," in *Acompañado a la comunidad* [Lima: CEP, 1982], p. 179).

8. I am thinking for example, of the forty Salvadorans killed during the celebration of the Eucharist on that day of real spiritual synthesis—Sunday, March 30, 1980—the day of Archbishop Romero's funeral.

9. Francis of Assisi showed insight when he linked poverty and humility together in his *Praises of the Virtues*: "Lady Holy Poverty, God keep you with your sister, holy Humility" (in M. A. Habig, ed., *St. Francis of Assisi: Writings and Early Biographies: Omnibus of Sources* [Chicago: Franciscan Herald Press, 1973], p. 132).

10. This attitude of availability to the Lord comes to the fore even in difficult and controversial situations. Without entering into detail here, let me put before the reader this expressive passage: "My dear Lord: It's been a long time since I've written. Today I really feel the need of you and your presence. Maybe it's because of the nearness of death or the relative failure of our struggle. You know I've always tried to be faithful to you in every way, consistent with the fulness of my being. That's why I'm here. I understand love as an urgent demand to solve the problem of the other—where you are.

"I left what I had and I came. Maybe today is my Holy Thursday and tonight will be my Good Friday. Into your hands I surrender completely all that I am with a trust having no limits, because I love you. What hurts me most is perhaps leaving behind those I love the most—Cecy and my family—and also not being able to experience the triumph of the people, its liberation. . . .

"I love you, and I give to you all that I am and all that we are, without measure—because you are my Father. . . .

"Ciao, Lord, perhaps until we meet in your heaven, that new land that we yearn for so much" (*My Life for My Friends: The Guerilla Journal of Néstor Paz, Christian* [Maryknoll, N.Y.: Orbis, 1975], p. 87).

11. "Mary sang this song that is now the song of the people, of the Christian people, and especially the people gathered in the Christian basic communities" (Bishop Sergio Méndez Arceo, homily on "María expresión suprema de lo feminino," in the Basilica of Guadalupe [May 26, 1982], in SVF, p. 137a).

Chapter 10

1. Dom Hélder Câmara says of this phenomenon: "The evident disproportion between the weakness of the basic communities and the immense twofold mission entrusted to them is proof that the Lord God is still exalting the humble" (address at a meeting of CELAM in Lima, Sept. 1975; published in SLE, p. 178a).

2. J. Hernández Pico, "La oración en los procesos latinoamericanos de liberación," in A. Cussiánovich et al., *Espiritualidad de la liberación* (Lima: CEP, 1980), pp. 181 and 183.

3. Ibid., p. 54.

4. "Ultimas reflexiones" (Sept. 1973), in SLE, pp. 235–36.

5. The text continues: "This is not 'until the next time'; this is goodbye forever. Greetings to our community. A fraternal greeting to all. Receive that greeting again when you exchange the kiss of peace in the community assembly. I will be present there because the church lives on and the Lord is present wherever two or more are gathered together. Your brother in Christ. P.S. My brevity and lack of clarity are due to the hour of affliction through which I am now passing; this is my Garden of Gethsemane" (letter of March 31, 1978, in *Nicaragua a un año de la victoria* [Lima: CEP, 1980], p. 109).

6. Homily, March 24, 1981, published in CRIE (Mexico City), March 23, 1981, p. 2.

7. Conclusions of the meeting at Vitória (Jan. 1975), in SLE, p. 314a. The priests of the archdiocese of San Salvador say something similar: "We know that in our weakness we depend on one another, and we glory that we are now more united than ever with a repressed faithful and a persecuted church. We are profoundly grateful for the support that the faithful give us in this option of ours that inspires us to serve them, and we ask forgiveness when our weakness flags behind our good desires and we do not serve as best we might" ("Opción preferencial por los pobres," in *El Salvador, un pueblo perseguido: Testimonios de cristianos* [Lima: CEP, 1980], p. 113).

8. Parish of Christ the Redeemer, "Celebramos nuestra fe" (in RIMAC, documentation service of the Instituto Bartolomé de Las Casas. These are communities formed by the power of love for God. "Love is not weakness or false complacency. It is the power of God. It is this Christian love that must inspire us to form strong communities in which we encourage one another to fulfill our obligations, defend our rights, and demand the promulgation and observance of just laws" (Bishop Gerardo Flores of Verapaz, "En el aniversario de los trágicos acontecimientos de Panzós" [May 29, 1979], in *Páginas*, 25 [Oct. 1979]: 68). Reflecting on the Fourth Meeting of the Basic Communities of Brazil, J. B. Libânio writes: "Struggle and hope: because God is with us. This is my summation of these four days" ("Elementos para una pastoral reflexión," in *Páginas*, 39 [Aug. 1981] 31).

9. Fourth International Congress of Theology, "Documento final," in *Páginas*, 28 (March 1980): 6; Eng. trans. in Sergio Torres and John Eagleson, eds., *The Challenge of Basic Christian Communities* (Maryknoll, N.Y.: Orbis Books, 1981), p. 241. "Nowhere is this liberating presence of Jesus Christ celebrated with greater joy and hope than in the ecclesial communities that have their basis in the people" ("América Latina: Evangelio," in *Páginas*, 19 [Jan. 1979]: 27). "Devotions" too are a celebration of the Lord's presence; see D. Irarrázaval, "Cristo Morado, Señor de los maltratados," in *Acompañando a la comunidad*, pp. 135–68.

10. Homily of Rutilio Grande at Apopa (Feb. 13, 1977), in SLE, p. 257ab, and in *El Salvador. Un pueblo perseguido*, p. 50. For this ecclesial outlook, see R. Muñoz, *La Iglesia en el pueblo* (Lima: CEP, 1983).

11. This sharing is a putting into practice of unity, which is always compatible with comradely criticism. Bishop Samuel Ruiz writes: "Jesus is manifested among us by unity in our labors. At the end of twenty years of episcopal service, I received the reassuring visit of brother bishops and theologians who also work among indigenous peoples and live in total commitment to proclaiming the truth that liberates: Christ committed by his blood to redeem humankind from all the oppressions it endures. Our sharing of experiences was rewarding, and their fraternal criticism was of incalculable value. I heard how others have borne with joy the consequences of preaching the gospel to the poor. It confirms fidelity to the Lord and to the church" (*Pastoral de Navidad* [Chiapas: San Cristóbal de Las Casas, 1979], p. 6).

12. See M. Martín del Blanco, *Santa Teresa de Jesús* (Bilbao: Mensajero, 1978), p. 103. There is another version of the famous saying of Teresa when she was dying, "Lord, I am a daughter of the church." But the meanings are essentially the same. I. Bengoechea. "¿Muero hija de la Iglesia?" in *Revista de espiritualidad* (Madrid, 1982), pp. 243–55, nn. 162–63, discusses the different transcription, exaggerating a little the different meanings.

INDEX OF SCRIPTURAL REFERENCES

OLD TESTAMENT

Genesis

2:7	152n.14
12:1	85

Exodus

3:7-8	77
3:18	77
5:1	74
6:2-8	73
6:7	78
18:20	81
19:5	11, 79

Numbers

14:4	76

Deuteronomy

6:22	84
8:2-6	75
8:7-10	77
8:11-14	79
8:14	77
10:14	11
11:10	74
11:12	79
30:15	70
30:19	29, 30

Psalms

9:1-2	19
9:9	19
14:4	60
16:11	100
33:1-3	19-20
33:5	19
42	24
42:5	18
42:11	24
43:3-4	24
85:3-4	100
85:6	100
107:5	76
125:1	106
128:1	79
133	132
137	11
137:6	130

Canticle of Canticles

8:7	110

Isaiah

5:8-9	79
40:3	76
61:1-2	43, 44
65:17-23	78, 121

Jeremiah

7:1-7	7
20:7	119-20
20:14-15	119
20:17-18	119
31:33	157n.12

Lamentations

3:22-23	99-100

Ezekiel

22:27	60
22:29	60

Hosea

2:14	85, 128

Micah

6:8	100

NEW TESTAMENT

Matthew

3:3	76
5:48	137
6:24	60
7:15-21	7
7:21	50
7:22	149n.14
8:20	41
8:34	150n.23
11:2-6	42-43, 45
11:3	46
11:25	30
12:50	41
14:27	105
16:14	48
16:16	149-50n.21
16:17	150n.21
18:3	127
25:31-46	38, 100, 104, 112

Mark

1:1	46
1:3	76
1:15	95
2:21-22	103
3:1-6	50
6:6-13	47
6:14-16	149n.20
8:27-35	45-51
8:33	50
10:35-45	49-50
15:34	131

Luke

1:1-4	36
1:46-48	111
1:46-55	127
1:47	152n.13
2:16-17	45
2:38	45

2:49	41
4:16-20	43
4:18	100
7:21	149n.14
9:20	149n.21
9:23	150n.26
9:61	40
10:29	34
10:36	34
15:18	34
18:18-23	40
18:22	95
24:5	30
24:39-43	155n.39

John

1:14	41
1:29	39
1:30	39
1:35-42	38-42
1:38	40
1:39	40, 41, 46, 148n.12
1:41	42, 43, 45
1:43	40
2:23-25	40
3:26	40
4:14	37
4:23	44
4:24	153n.19
4:28	45
6:65	35
7:38	37
7:39	148n.8
8:12	40
8:32	88
8:33-36	76
10:4	40
10:10	154n.35
10:18	92, 169n.7

12:26	40
13:26	40
14:1	157n.13
14:6	157n.13
15:12	142n.18
15:15	33
15:16	35, 38
15:20	40
16:13	55, 88
20:17-18	38, 45
20:31	46
21:9	40
21:24	36

Acts

2:36	46
2:41-47	52
9:1-5	80
9:2	156n.7
13:10	156n.8
13:12	156n.8
16:17	81, 156n.8
18:25	81
18:25-26	156n.8
18:26	81
19:9	81
19:23	81
22:4	80
22:7-8	80-81
24:14	81
24:22	81
26:9	81

Romans

1:3	57
1:9	62
3:20	56
5:15	109
5:17	71
6:4	157n.12
6:5	66-67

6:6	65, 67	*1 Corinthians*		2:13	61
6:9	68	1:26	57	2:17	57
6:12	65	1:29	56	3:17	68, 70
6:14	68, 82	2:4	64	4:10-11	65, 69
6:19	57	3:1	63	4:11	57
7:4	68, 69	4:16	81	4:12	69
7:5	68	4:17	81	6:2	8, 20
7:15	61	5:3	62, 65	6:7	64
7:24	65, 67	6:13	66	7:1	62
8	55	6:14	66	7:5	56, 119
8:1	58-59, 64	6:15	68	7:13	62
8:1-10	154n.36	6:17	63	8:1-5	120
8:2	63-64, 82	6:18	65	8:8	109
8:3	58, 63, 64	6:19	67	10:2	57
8:4	3, 33, 54, 55,	7:4	65	12:7	56
	60, 63, 67, 83	7:28	56	*Galatians*	
8:5	58	7:34	62	2:10	44, 124
8:6	59, 63, 64	8:13	151n.4	2:16	56
8:7	59	9:19	92	4:6	63
8:8	58	9:27	65	4:13	57
8:9	59, 64	12	53	4:14	56
8:10	61, 63, 68	12:4-6	64	5	55
8:11	67	12:7	63	5:1	22, 82, 92
8:12	59	12:27	68	5:13	34, 58, 82, 92
8:13	59, 65	12:31	72, 82	5:16	63
8:14	71	13	62	5:17	58
8:15	62, 63	13:3	65	5:18	64, 82
8:16	63	13:7-8	82	5:19-21	59
8:17	71	13:8	152n.16	5:20	59
8:21	3, 34	13:12	72	5:21	59
8:23	63, 67-68	14:1	62	5:22	86
8:26	64, 71	14:12	53	5:22-23	62, 152n.16
8:37	70	15:26	154n.35	5:23	91
8:38	70	15:39	56	5:25	63
9:5	57	15:44	66, 67	6:17	65
12:1	67	15:50	68	6:18	62
12:4-5	69	15:55-57	121	*Ephesians*	
14:21	151n.4	15:56	68	1:3-5	110
15:26	109	16:18	61	1:22-23	68-69
15:30	62	*2 Corinthians*		4:14	105
16:8	60	1:12	57, 60	5:5	60
16:25-26	71	1:17	57	5:28	56

Philippians		2:11	65	2:14	91
1:8	162n.24	3:5	60	2:26	91
1:20	67	1 Thessalonians		1 John	
1:22	56	5:19	91	1:1-4	44-45
2:5	96	2 Timothy		4:8	45
3:18-19	60	1:7	62	4:18	45
3:21	67	4:22	61	4:19	109
4:23	62	Philemon		5:12	45
Colossians		16	56	Revelation	
1:22	65	Hebrews		3:18	26
1:24	56, 116	11	85	3:20	20, 52, 136
2:1	56	James		5:8-9	39-40
2:5	56, 62, 65	2:5	91		
2:6	82	2:12	91		

INDEX OF NAMES AND SOURCES

Albert the Great, 52
Alfaro, Juan, 156
Alsina, Juan, 130
Alvarez Calderón, Jorge, 160, 169
Alvear, Bishop Enrique, 162
Andrés, M., 150
Angelelli, Bishop Enrique, 120-21, 167-68
Anselm, Saint, 36
Antoine, Charles, 164
Antoncich, R., 160
Aquinas, Thomas, 36, 52, 92, 110
Arguedas, José María, 21, 139, 152
Arrupe, Pedro, 141-42, 161
Ascent of Mount Carmel (John of the Cross), 33, 83-88
Aubert, R., 142
Augustine, Saint, 70, 77, 83, 88, 109, 152
Bambaren, Bishop Luis, 166
Barth, Karl, 154
Bengochea, I., 171
Berdyaev, Nikolai, 162
Bernanos, Georges, 111, 167
Bernard of Clairvaux, Saint, 5, 37
Betto, Frei, 164
Boff, Leonardo, 138, 146, 165, 166
Boismard, M. E., 148
Bonaventure, Saint, 53
Bonhoeffer, Dietrich, 159
Bonnard, P., 151, 152

Bonnín, E., 154-55
Borreto, J., 148nn.10, 12; 149n.13
Bouyer, L., 140, 145, 154
Bover, J. M., 151
Brockman, James R., 140
Brown, R. E., 148
Bultmann, Rudolf, 153nn.24, 28; 154
Burnier, João-Bosco, 118
Caba, J., 148
Cabestrero, T., 145
Câmara, Dom Hélder, 144, 170
Cano, Bishop Valencia, 143
Cano, Melchior, 150
Casaldáliga, Bishop Pedro, 118, 144-45, 166, 167
Cathenet, E., 148
Cerfaux, L., 154, 163
Chenu, M.-D., 129, 147
CLAI (Consejo Latinoamericano de Iglesias), 154
CLAR (Confederación Latino-americana de Religiosos), 123, 140n.14, 141n.15, 163
Coll, Pilar, 166
Comblin, J., 148
Conference of Religious of Guatemala, 105, 162
Conference of Religious of Puerto Rico, 140
Congar, Yves, 140, 148
Constitutions of the Society of

Jesus, The (Ignatius of Loyola), 87
Cullmann, Oscar, 148
Cussiánovich, A., 164, 165, 169, 170
Dalle, Bishop Luis, 139, 168
Dammert, Bishop José, 164-65
de Guibert, J., 142, 150, 151, 159, 163
De Jonge, M., 148
del Blanco, M. Martín, 171
Delorme, J., 157
Diez, María del Carmen, 163
Dives in Misericordia. See Encyclicals
Dominic Guzmán, Saint, 26, 52, 169
Duplacy, J., 157
Dupont, J., 149, 157
Duquoc, C., 157
Dussel, E., 144
Duvalier, J. C., 140
Eagleson, John, 171
Echegaray, Hugo, 118, 146-47, 153-54, 163
Elizondo, Virgilio, 157-58
Encyclicals: *Dives in Misericordia (Rich in Mercy),* 149, 155; *Laborem Exercens (On Human Work),* 143, 161, 162; *Redemptor Hominis (Redeemer of the Human Race),* 157
Episcopal Conference of El Salvador, 161
Episcopal Conference of Guatemala, 101, 116, 124, 166
Episcopal Conference of Peru, 98
Erdozaín, Plácido, 147
Espinal, Luis, 117, 125, 158, 165
Estrada, Bishop Luis María, 166, 168
Fabella, Virginia, 138

Fessard, G., 163
Feuillet, A., 154
Flores, Bishop Gerardo, 171
Fourth International Congress of Theology, 171
Fourth Meeting of the Christians of Puno (Peru), 160, 163
Francis de Sales, Saint, 88, 140
Francis of Assisi, Saint, 26, 53, 147, 169
Galilea, Segundo, 138
Gallego, Héctor, 162
García Márquez, Gabriel, 27, 130
Gelabert, M., 146
Gelin, A., 157
George, A., 148
Gilleman, G., 142
Gilson, E., 138
Girardi, Bishop, 117
Gonzales Dávila, Gil, 144
González, Ruiz, J. M., 152
Gottwald, Norman, 156
Grande, Rutilio, 103, 134, 162, 166, 171
Grelot, P., 148
Gremillion, J., 159
Guillet, Jacques, 153
Gutiérrez, Gustavo, 138nn.1, 5; 139; 143nn.1, 4; 144; 146; 147; 150; 153; 158; 159; 160nn.1, 2, 3; 163; 165nn.14, 15
Guy, J. C., 143
Habig, M. A., 169
Hernández Pico, Juan, 164, 166, 170
Hondarza, Vincente, 162
Huby, J., 153
Iblacker, Reinhold, 145, 162
Ignatius of Loyola, Saint: as connecting freedom and love, 160; difficulties with theologians of, 150; as emphasizing

effective action, 108, 109; on freedom and spirituality, 87; on God as in all things, 110; historical context of the spirituality of, 26-27; as a "poor pilgrim," 158; spiritual experiences of, 52, 53, 147; as synthesizing the contemplative and active, 143

Innocent III, 26

Irarrázaval, D., 171

John of the Cross, Saint, 158, 162; historical context of the spirituality of, 27; on spirituality and freedom, 33; the spirituality of, 83-88; as emphasizing self-giving, 110; on solitude and spirituality, 129, 131

John Paul II, 149; on Archbishop Romero, 165; on the church's solidarity with workers, 102, 143, 161n.14; on the early experience of the Jewish people, 155; on interpreting the Bible, 160; on Jesus as the "way," 157; on the Puebla Document, 98; on the spirituality of work, 162; on the "structures of sin," 161n.5. *See also* Encyclicals

John the Baptist, 39, 40, 42, 43, 44, 45, 47, 48

John XXIII, 22, 29

Kempis, Thomas à, 148

Laborem Exercens. See Encyclicals

Lagrange, M. J., 150nn.23, 27; 152

Laínez, Diego, 53

Lamarche, P., 154

Landázuri, Cardinal Juan, 98, 115-16

Lange, Martin, 145, 162

Las Casas, Bartolomé de, 30, 162

Latin American Conference of Religious. *See* CLAR

Latin American Council of Churches (CLAI), 154

Le Dû, C., 154

Legido López, M., 163

Leonardi, C., 140

Leon-Dufour, X., 151nn.7, 9; 153

Libânio, J. B., 138, 171

Lumen Gentium, 55

Lyonnet, S., 156, 157nn.12, 15

Machado de Asís, Joaquín María, 3

Manicardi, E., 148

Marchel, W., 153

Marguerat, D., 152

Márquez, Gabriel García. *See* García Márquez, Gabriel

Mateos, J., 148nn.10, 12; 149n.13

Medellín (Second General Conference of the Latin American Episcopate), 161, 168; on injustice as sinful, 97-98; on "institutionalized violence," 9; on poverty, 141; on solidarity with the poor and rejection of poverty, 123, 124, 143; on spiritual poverty, 127; on structural causes of poverty, 122; on unjust structures, 116

Méndez Arceo, Bishop Sergio, 132-33, 170

Metz, J. B., 159

Milagro, J. M., 146

Mollat, M., 146

Moses, 73, 77

Muñoz, R., 171

Nadal, Jerónimo, 53

National Conference of the Religious of Nicaragua, 168

Neher, A., 155-56
Nolan, Albert, 151
Nouwen, Henri, 164
O'Callaghan, J., 151
Octogesima Adveniens, 159
On Human Work. See Encyclicals
ONIS (Oficina Nacional de Investigación Social), 146
Ossio, Juan, 139
Paoli, A., 138
Partelli, Archbishop Carlos, 143
Paul VI, 159
Paz, Néstor, 169-70
Pereira Neto, Henrique, 144
Pironio, Cardinal E., 138
Poma de Ayala, F. Guamán, 139, 152, 162
Pons, Jacques, 155
Potterie, I. de la, 148
Proaño, Bishop Leonidas, 103
Puebla Document (Final Document of the Third General Conference of the Latin American Episcopate): on basic ecclesial communities, 128; on Christ in the poor, 38, 99; on evangelization and struggle, 145; on evangelization by the poor, 30; on injustice as sinful, 98, 160-61; on liberation for communion, 92; on living alongside the poor, 141; on poverty, 9; on the "preferential option for the poor," 101; on solidarity with the poor and rejection of poverty, 122-23; on the "spirituality of evasion," 15; on structural causes of poverty, 99, 122; on suffering in Latin America, 139
Rahner, Karl, 145, 166

*Redeemer of the Human Race.
See* Encyclicals
Redemptor Hominis. See Encyclicals
Ribadaneira, Pedro, 163
Richard, P., 154
Rich in Mercy. See Encyclicals
Riera, J., 160
Robinson, J. A. T., 151, 153 nn.25, 27; 154
Romero, Archbishop Oscar Arnulfo, 140, 167n.13, 169; on the church in the world, 147; on his conversion by and resurrection in the poor, 32; on conversion and struggle against injustice, 98; on effective action and love, 108; on giving hope to the poor, 25, 145-46; on hope and struggle, 105; John Paul II on, 165; poem on the death of, 144-45; as seeking solitude and communion, 132-33; on sin as the cause of death, 99; on suffering leading to radical reforms, 166-67; suspicions about, 12
Rose, Juan Gonzalo, 163-64
Ruiz, Bishop Samuel, 171
Saint-Exupéry, Antoine de, 111
Schillebeeckx, Edward, 147
Schlier, H., 152
Schmitz, Bishop Germán, 124
Schnackenburg, R., 149, 160
Second Vatican Council. *See* Vatican II
Sobrino, Jon, 138, 140, 169
Tamez, Elsa, 155
Taylor, V., 149
Teresa of Avila, Saint, 27, 88, 106, 111, 135, 163

Thérèse of Lisieux, Saint, 88, 111
Thils, G., 142, 161
Tillesse, G. Minette de, 149,
    150nn.22, 25
Tissot, J., 141, 142
Torres, Gilmer, 165
Torres, Sergio, 138, 171
Tutu, Bishop Desmond, 166

Valdivieso, Bishop Antonio, 144
Vallejos, Bishop Luis, 156
Vatican II, 22, 47, 102, 128, 161
Vicaire, M.-H., 169
Wrede, W., 149
Zegarra, Bishop Martín, 162
Zevallos, N., 138
Zumstein, J., 148

Other Orbis books . . .

Gutiérrez, Gustavo
THE POWER OF THE POOR IN HISTORY

"This is a people's theology, not a textbook theology . . . addressed not to professional theologians but to lay people. . . . This is not a theology created by the intelligentsia, the affluent, the powerful, those on top; it is a theology from the bottom, from 'the underside,' created by the victims, the poor, the oppressed. It is not theology spun out in a series of principles or axioms of timeless truth that are then applied to the contemporary scene, but a theology springing up out of the poverty, the oppression, the heartrending conditions under which the great majority of Latin Americans lives."

Robert McAfee Brown, from the Preface

"The essence of his theology of liberation is evangelical militant compassion, a truly theological project based on the very core of the Gospel. He is the first person in modern history to re-actualize the great Christian themes of theology, starting from a fundamental option for the poor. This new way of theologizing does not just add a new chapter to the old theology—it conceptualized not only the pastoral and institutional aspects of Christian ecclesial life but also its dogmatic and ethical aspects, in a way long-forgotten in Europe." *Edward Schillebeeckx*

ISBN 0-88344-388-0 *272pp. Paper $10.95*

A THEOLOGY OF LIBERATION (9th Printing)

"Over the past ten years an estimated 15,000 new religious books have been published. The Protestant weekly *Christian Century* asked 89 of its scholarly reviewers which titles from the 70s 'most deserve to survive.' (*A Theology of Liberation* was sixth in the order of votes received.) This book is a bible for a generation of Third World theorists.'' *Time Magazine*

"Rarely does one find such a happy fusion of gospel content and contemporary relevance.'' *The Lutheran Standard*

"Has practically become required reading among U.S. missionaries and church bureaucrats.'' *The Wall Street Journal*

"This is one of the most acute and the most readable theological essays of today on the meaning and mission of the Church.''
Catholic Library World

ISBN 0-88344-477-1   *334pp. Cloth $7.95*
ISBN 0-88344-478-X   *Paper $6.95*

Cardenal, Ernesto
THE GOSPEL IN SOLENTINAME
(four volumes)

"Farmers and fishermen in a remote village in Nicaragua join their priest for dialogues on Bible verses. Here is a translation (earthy epithets intact) of the tape-recorded conversations. Highly recommended to confront the complacent with the stark realities of religious and political consciousness in the Third World.'' *Library Journal*

ISBN 0-88344-176-4   *Vol. 1, 288pp. Paper $8.95*
ISBN 0-88344-175-6   *Vol. 2, 272pp. Paper $8.95*
ISBN 0-88344-174-8   *Vol. 3, 320pp. Paper $8.95*
ISBN 0-88344-173-X   *Vol. 4, 288pp. Paper $8.95*

Scharper, Philip and Sally, eds.
THE GOSPEL IN ART BY THE PEASANTS OF SOLENTINAME

Thirty-one stunning, full-color prints of Nicaraguan peasants' depictions of the gospel stories. The texts facing each painting are commentaries of the peasants on the Gospel passage relating to that painting. No other time or place offers us such a detailed and comprehensive record of what "ordinary" Christians made of the Gospel in the context of their own lives.

ISBN 0-88344-382-1   *Cloth $9.95*

Galilea, Segundo
THE BEATITUDES
To Evangelize as Jesus Did

An inspirational treatment of the Beatitudes of both Luke and Matthew by a popular writer of spirituality.

"Long experience in pastoral activity has qualified Galilea, one of Latin America's best-known theologians, to direct others on the way to spiritual maturity. His message is written in a style that makes sense to anyone, lay or expert, ready to give assent to the radical challenge of the Gospel." *Spirituality Today*

The warmth and openness with which Galilea preaches this gospel should inspire the activist to prayer, the pious to action, and all of us to a deeper reliance on the roots of our faith." *Sojourners*
ISBN 0-88344-344-9 *128pp. Paper $5.95*

FOLLOWING JESUS (2nd Printing)

" 'In the language of the Gospel, a radical is one who goes to the root of things, one who accepts the teachings of Jesus with all their consequences,' argues the Chilean theologian who issues this passionate summons to Christian radicalism. His christology, based mainly on the synoptic gospels, stresses Jesus' earthly ministry, especially in its social and political dimensions. Admonishing Christians to follow Jesus' ministry to the poor and oppressed, and advocating a life of contemplation and prayer, he presents Mary as the ideal follower of Jesus. This popular treatment, accessible to lay readers, is recommended for general and church libraries as a representative example of Latin American liberation theology." *Library Journal*
ISBN 0-88344-136-5 *128pp. Paper $5.95*

Cabestrero, Teofilo
MINISTERS OF GOD,
MINISTERS OF THE PEOPLE
Testimonies of Faith from Nicaragua

Extensive interviews with Ernesto Cardenal, Minister of Culture, Fernando Cardenal, Youth Movement Coordinator, and Miguel d'Escoto, Foreign Minister. These three priests in the Nicaraguan government explain how they combine their priesthood and their political commitment.

"I used to watch these padres in government at some of their meetings. And I would ask myself, What are they thinking and feeling? What is going on inside them? What is their interior experience in all this—their faith, their pain, their hope, their fears, their temptations? They have, of course, their own personal stories, their sensitivities, their reasoning, their wounds, their emotions, their desires, their hopes. And I said to myself that there must be, in each of them, a given quantity of generosity, of faith, of sin perhaps, and conversion, too. I have obtained the personal testimony of three of them. And I offer this testimony, with all my heart, to the world, in the conviction that, wherever we have a sincere witness to love, faith, service, and sacrifice, there we have a revelation—a revelation of God, a revelation of the gospel, a revelation of truth, life, and meaning."—*From the Introduction*

Teofilo Cabestrero is a Spanish priest-journalist now working in Nicaragua.

ISBN 0-88344-335-X   *144pp. Paper $6.95*

Bavarel, Michel
NEW COMMUNITIES, NEW MINISTRIES
The Church Resurgent in Africa, Asia, and Latin America

This book is a journalist's account of small Christian communities in a variety of cultural and geographical settings throughout the Third World. The vitality of the young churches is dramatically portrayed as a picture of the Church as the Church must increasingly become. Through this portrayal, the challenge for the First World is eminently clear.

Christians can never be anything except "people of the universal church." Right from the start the disciples headed for the ends of the earth, and for the outermost bounds of their own selves. This is a book of living witness. It teems with the witness of the new countries, the "young Churches" that live the Gospel today in the Third World, in another culture, and in a situation of poverty as their daily lot.

ISBN 0-88344-337-6   *128pp. Paper $5.95*